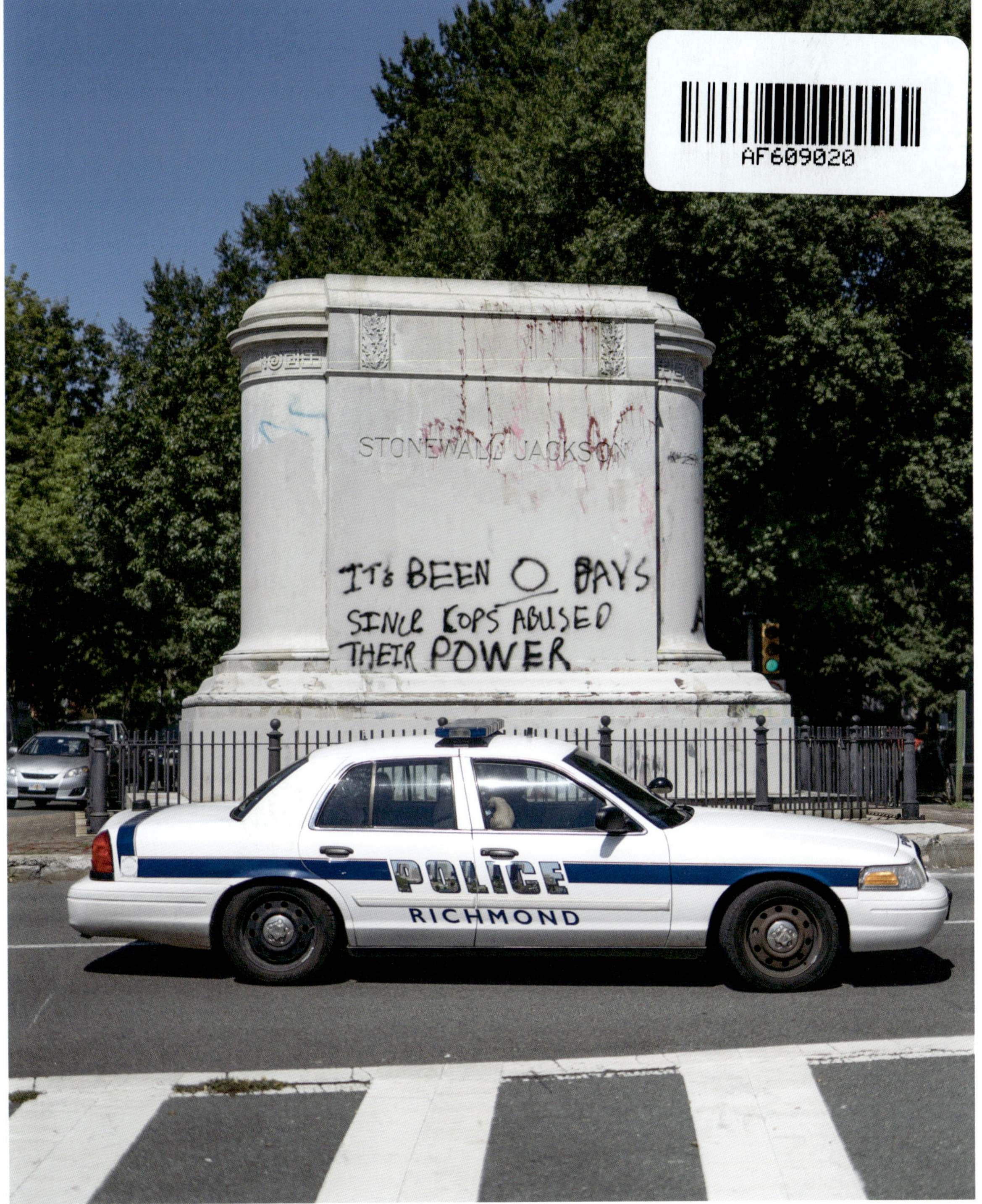
STONEWALL JACKSON
IT's BEEN 0 DAYS
SINCE COPS ABUSED
THEIR POWER
POLICE
RICHMOND

Fall of 2020 saw the intersection of the covid-19 pandemic, a looming presidential election and mass protests against atrocities committed by the police state. The election would be preceded by 3 Presidential debates to be held in Cleveland, Miami and Nashville.

Starting in Cleveland, I would set out on a month long road trip to photograph at and in between each of the debates. Culminating in a final trip to Pennsylvania on Election Day. My only guidelines were to abstain from breaching any press Barriers at the debates, I would instead experience them amidst the protests, rallies and unsettling moments between.

Although grounded in the parameters of engaging the debates, the work ended up being more about the spaces between the tension. The empty city scapes, the quiet country sides, the moments to connect with another person and hear their story. I'd like to think I made some of my most disdainful photographs as well as some of my most joyous portraits. To photograph a stranger in those months was not only about responding to them, but experiencing social connection again after 7 months of seclusion.

In the end, the work serves as a documentary mode response to a time when many of us felt shut off, shut out and incapable of effecting change. As a photographer, my desire was to create a visual narrative that portrayed what I experienced in that time, versus what we were fed on the screens and in print.

+ Marshall Scheuttle

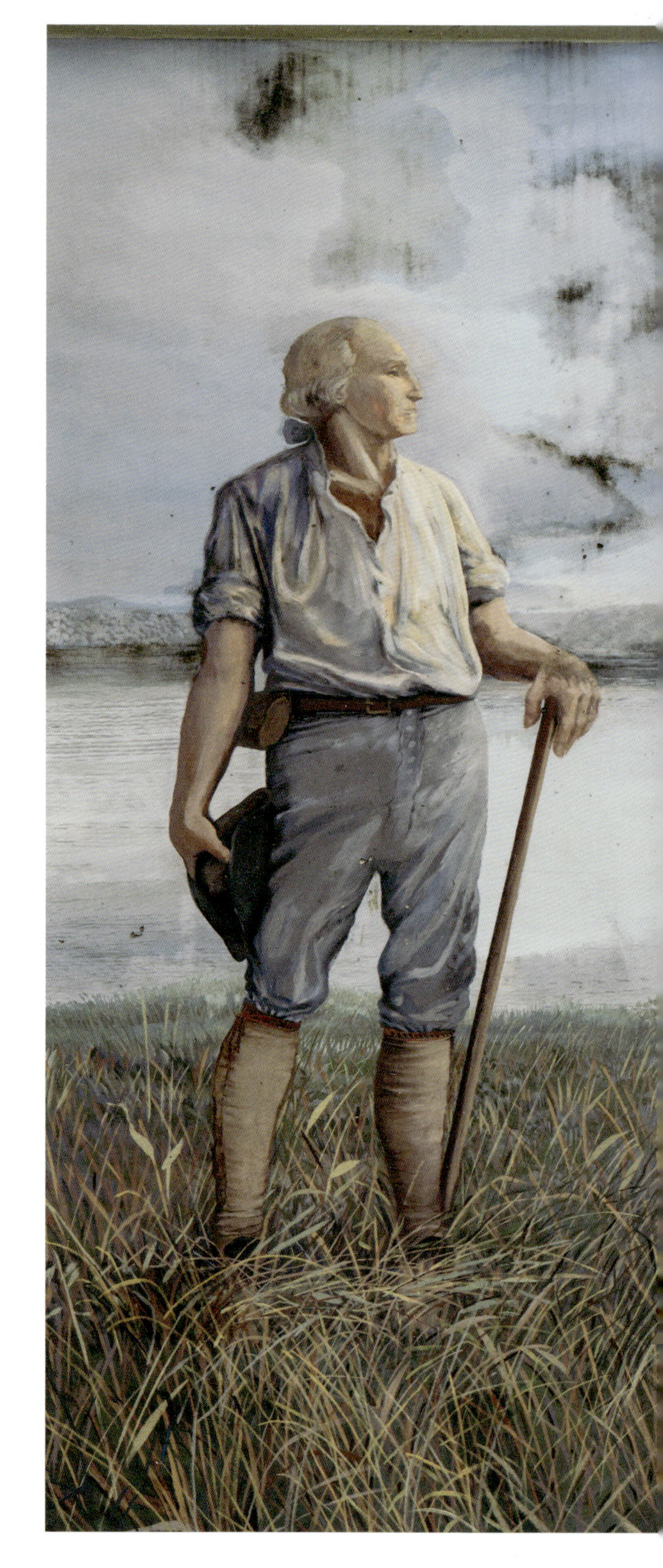

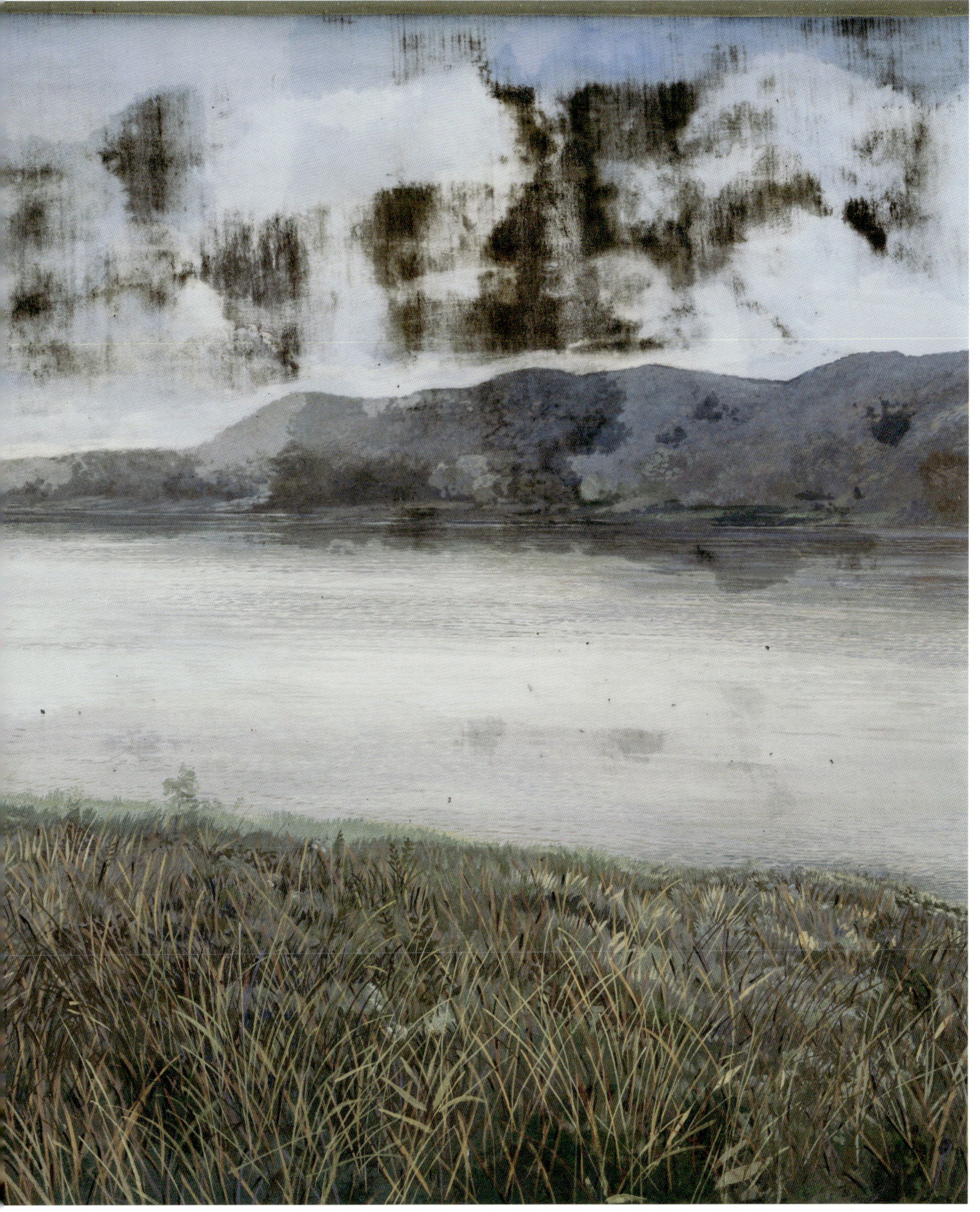

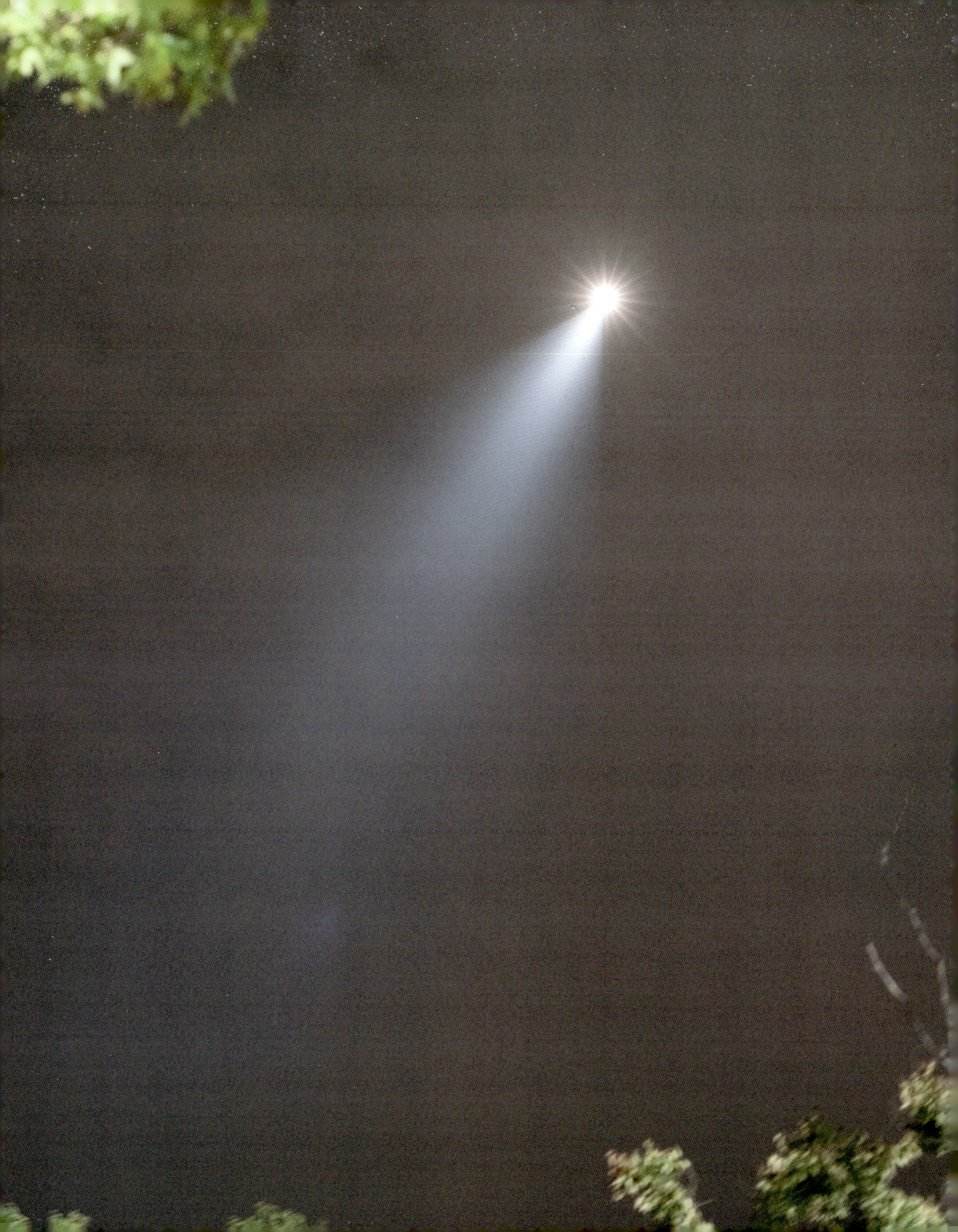

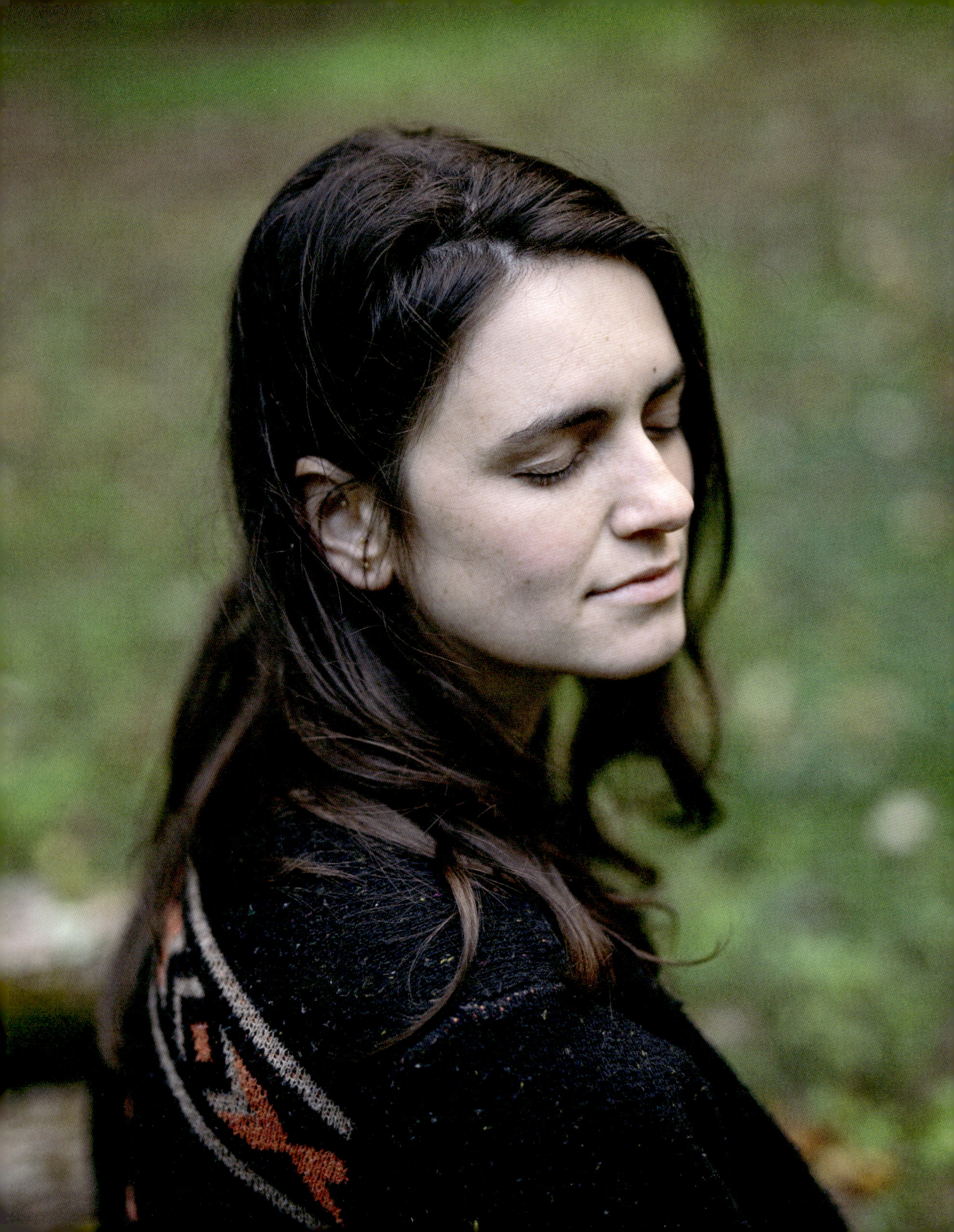

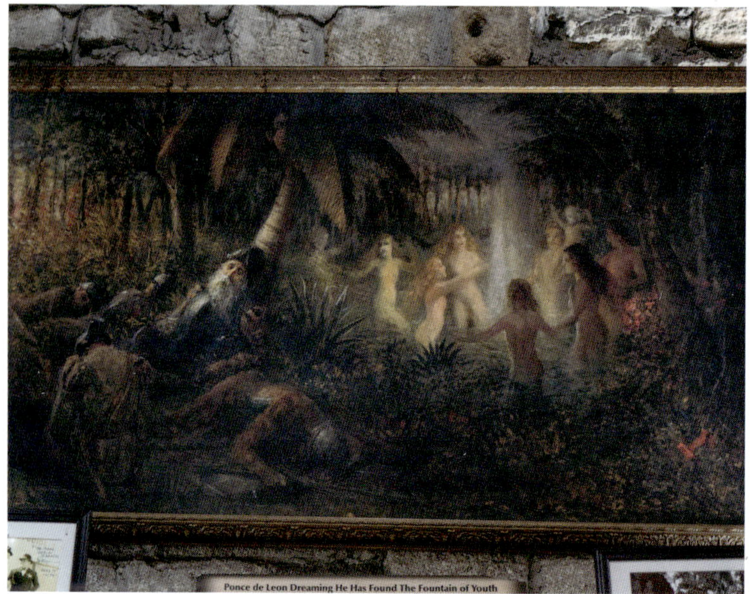
Ponce de Leon Dreaming He Has Found The Fountain of Youth

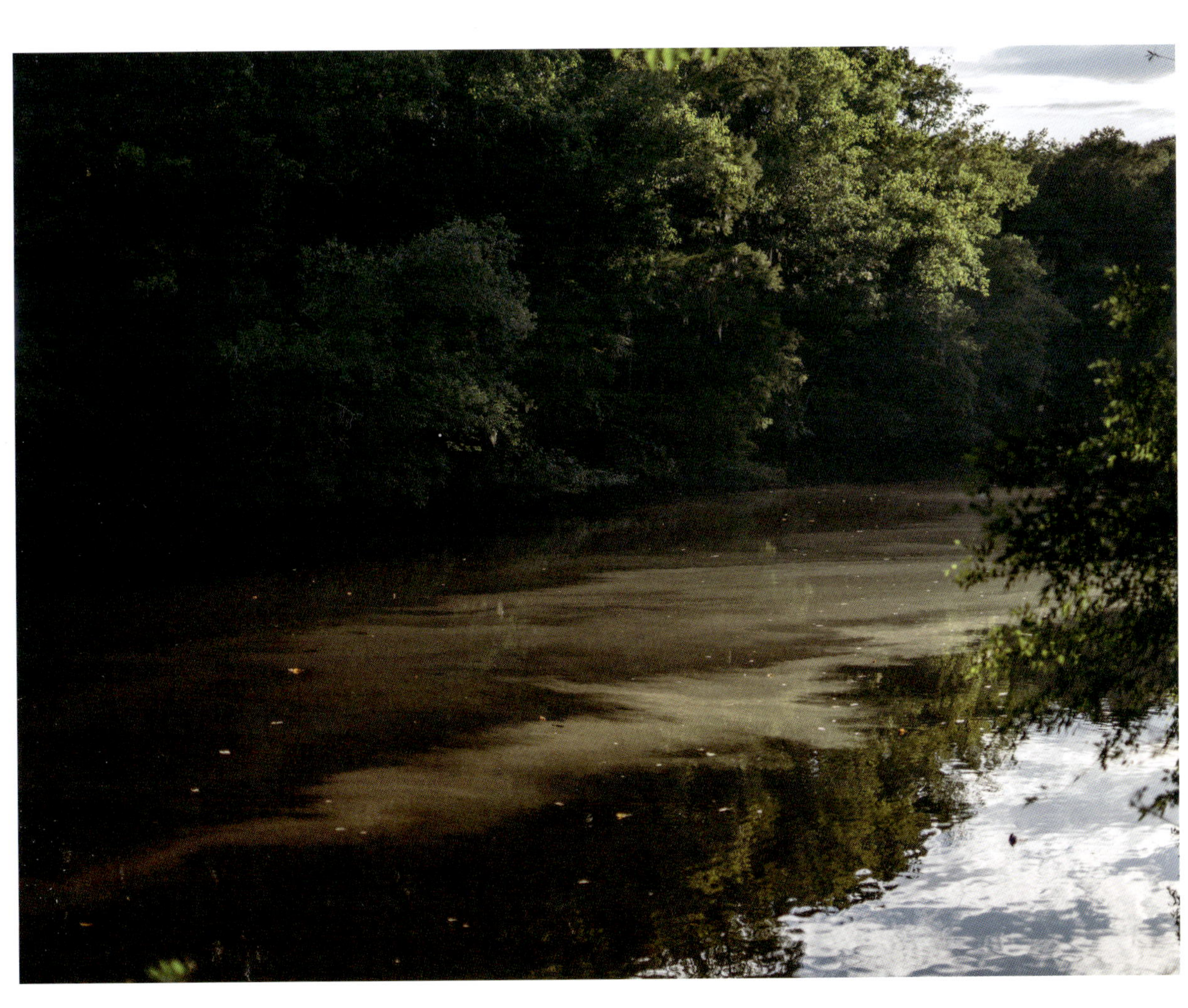

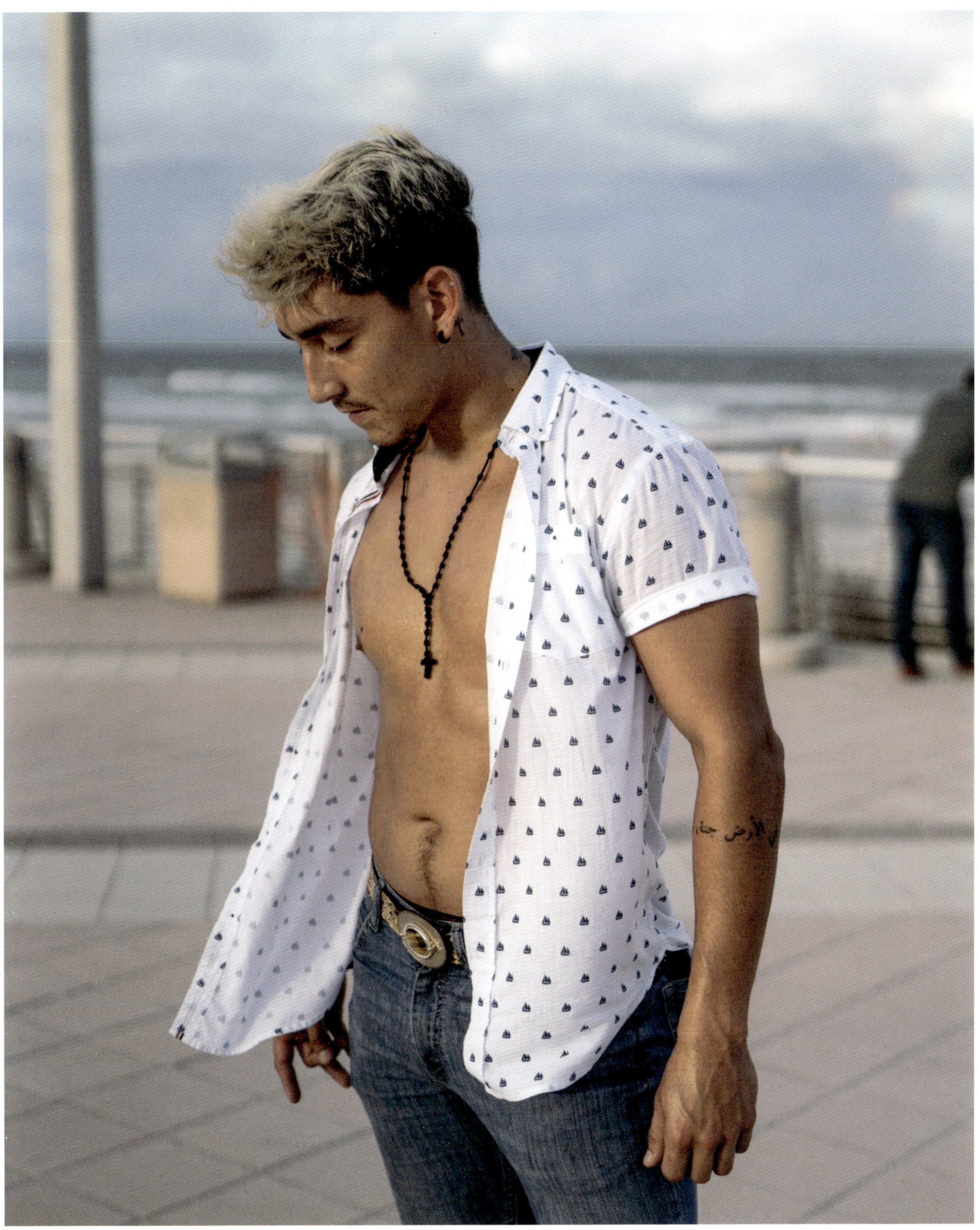

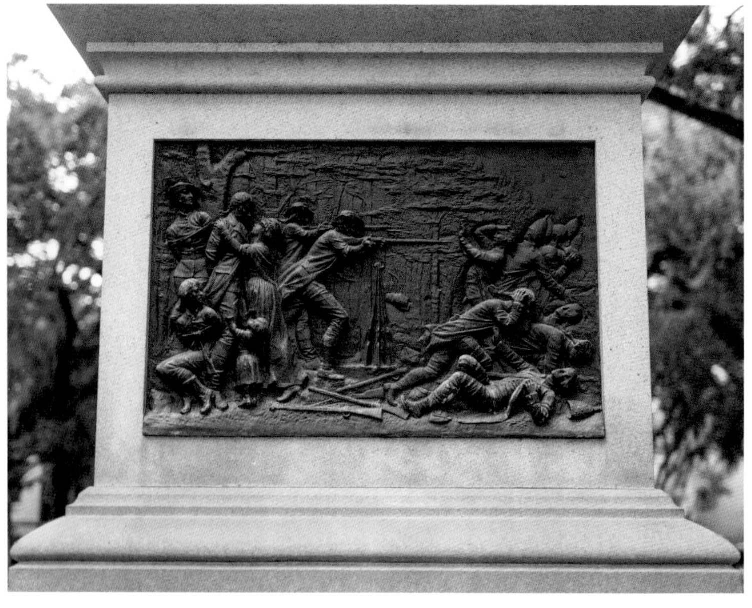

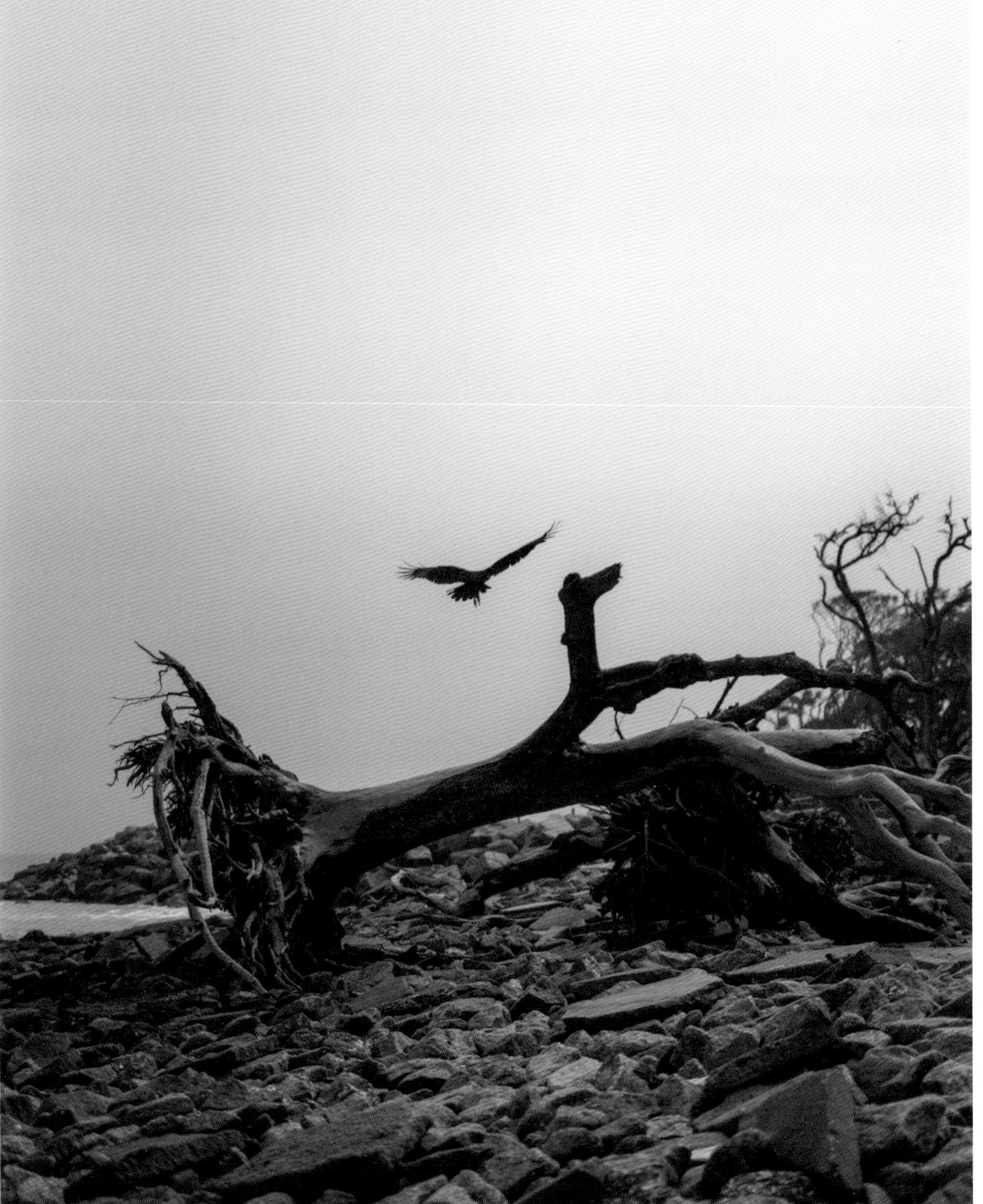

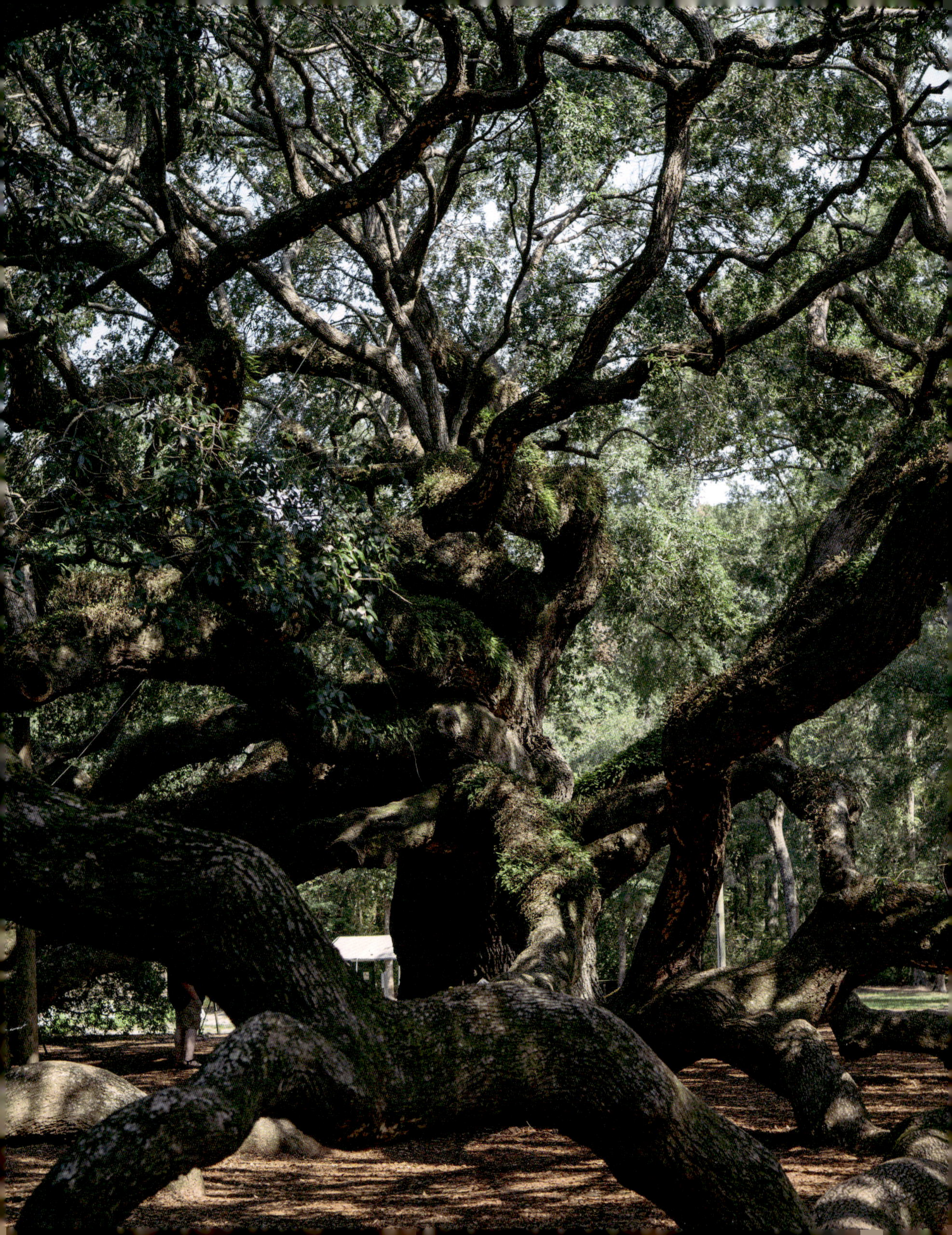

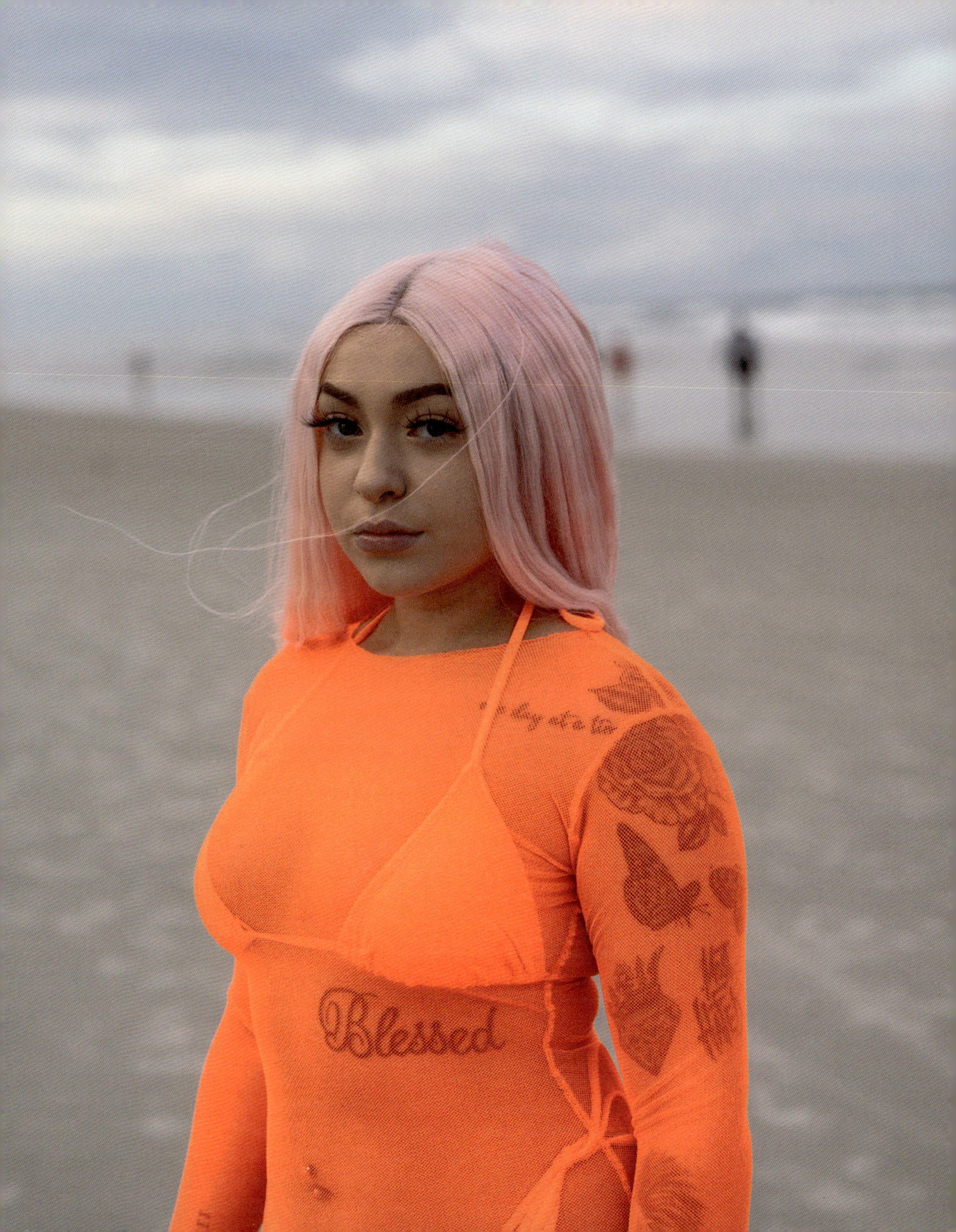
Blessed

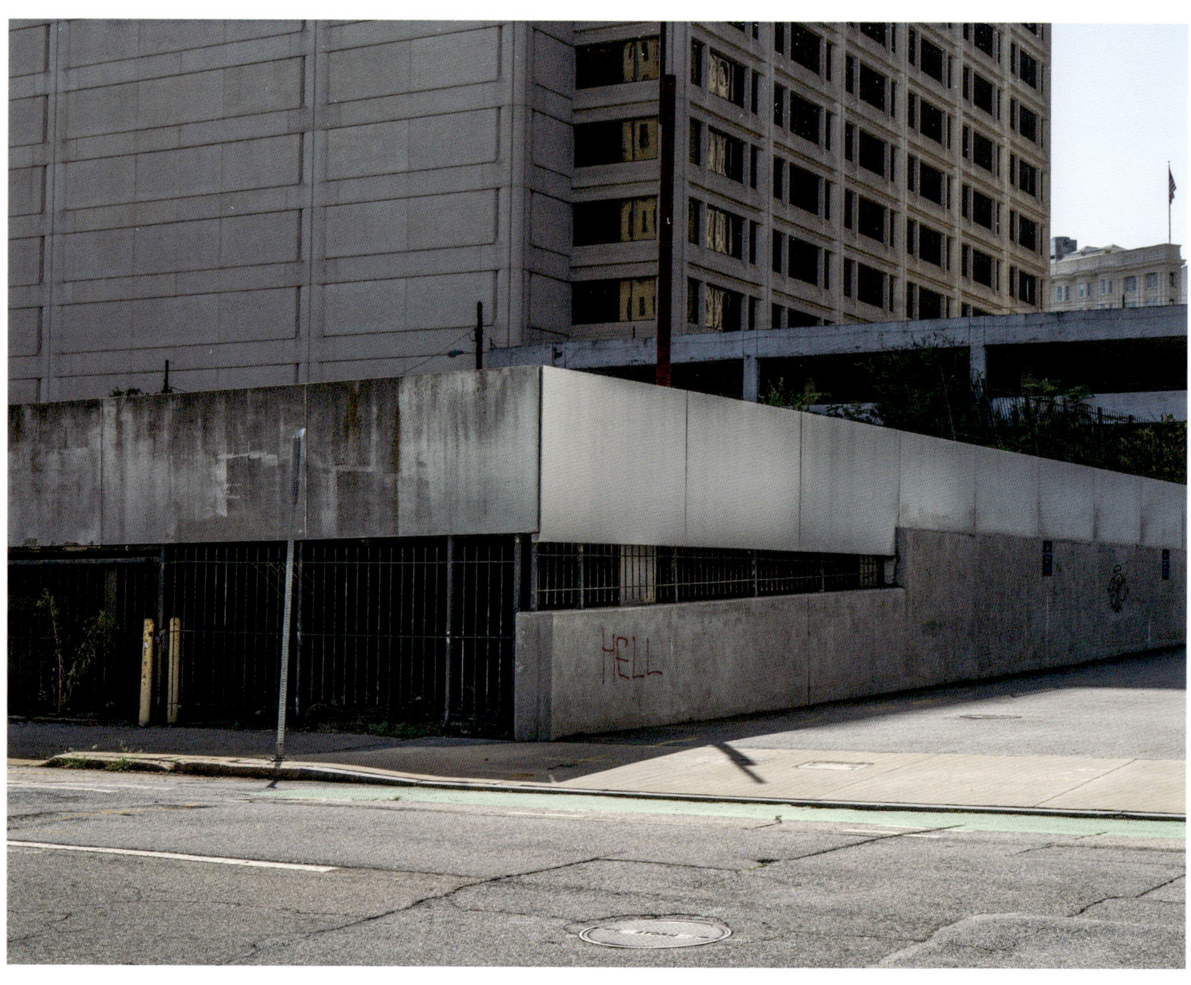
HELL

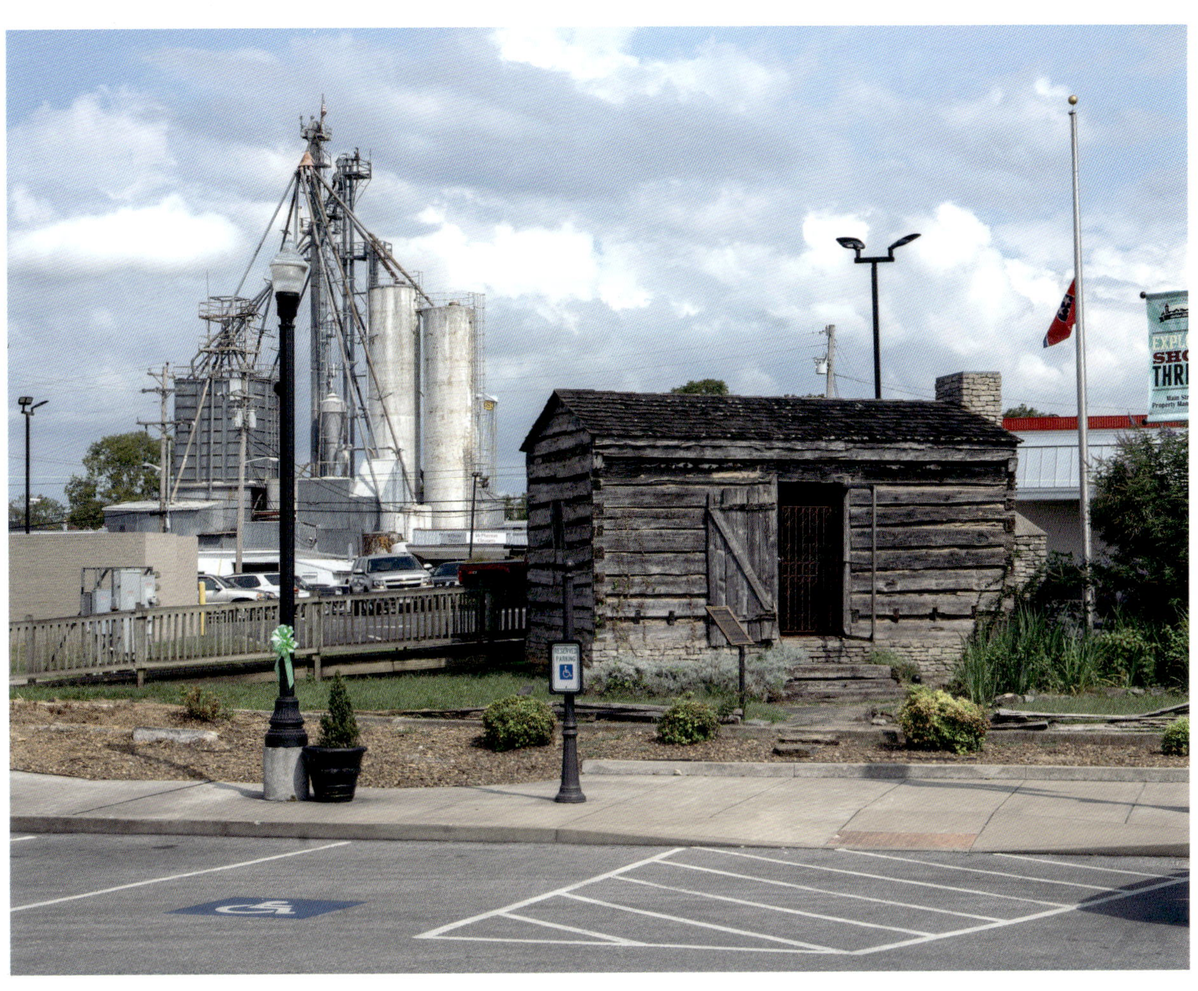
RESERVED
PARKING

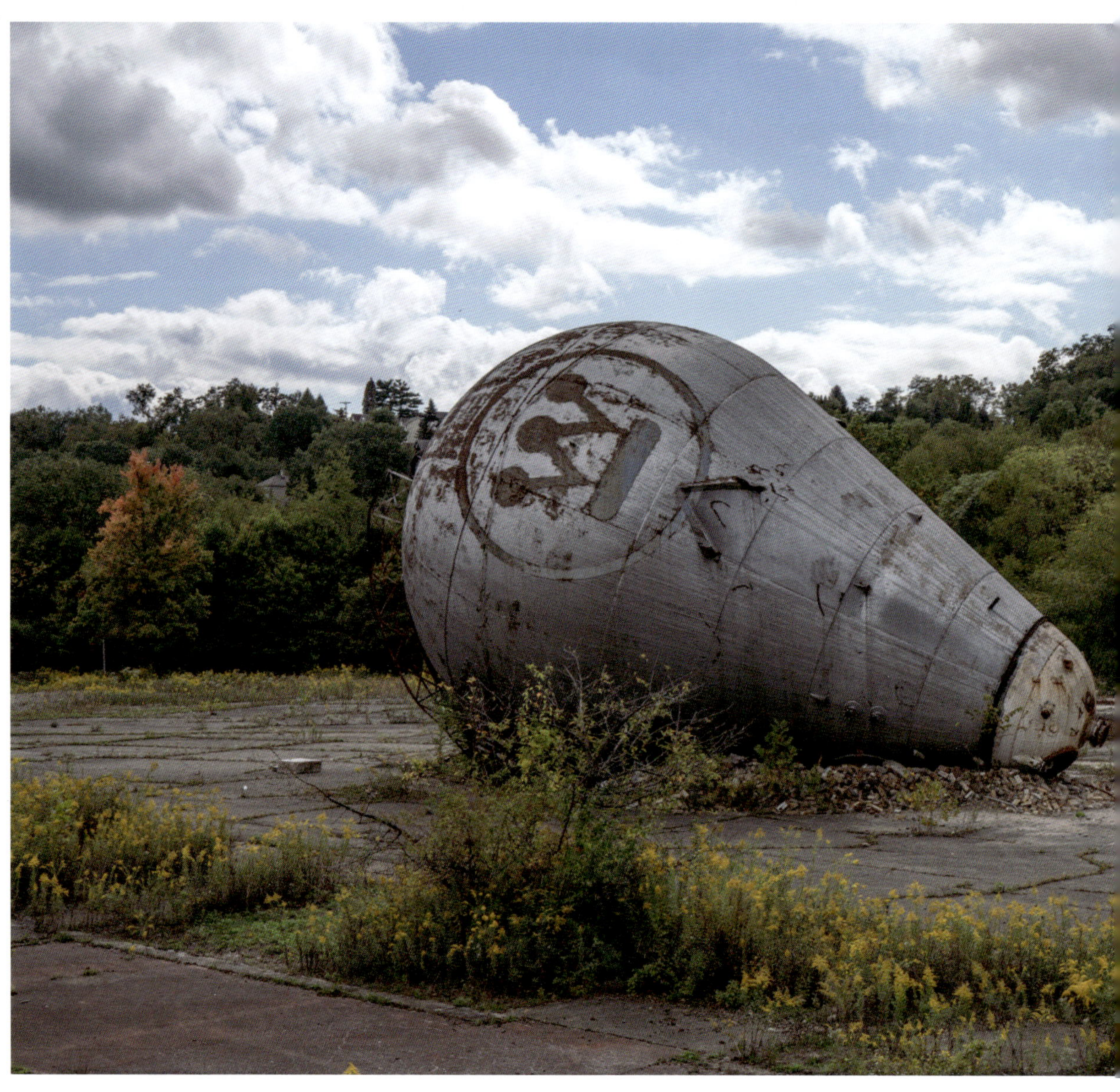

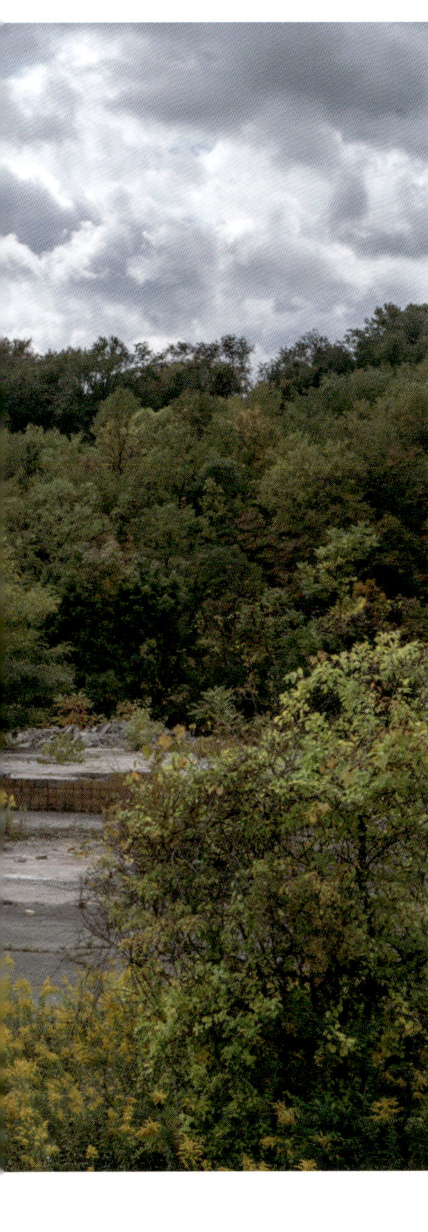

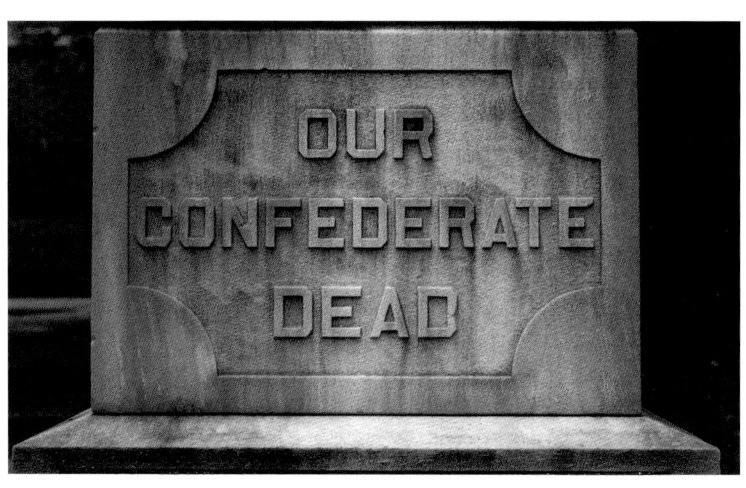
OUR
CONFEDERATE
DEAD

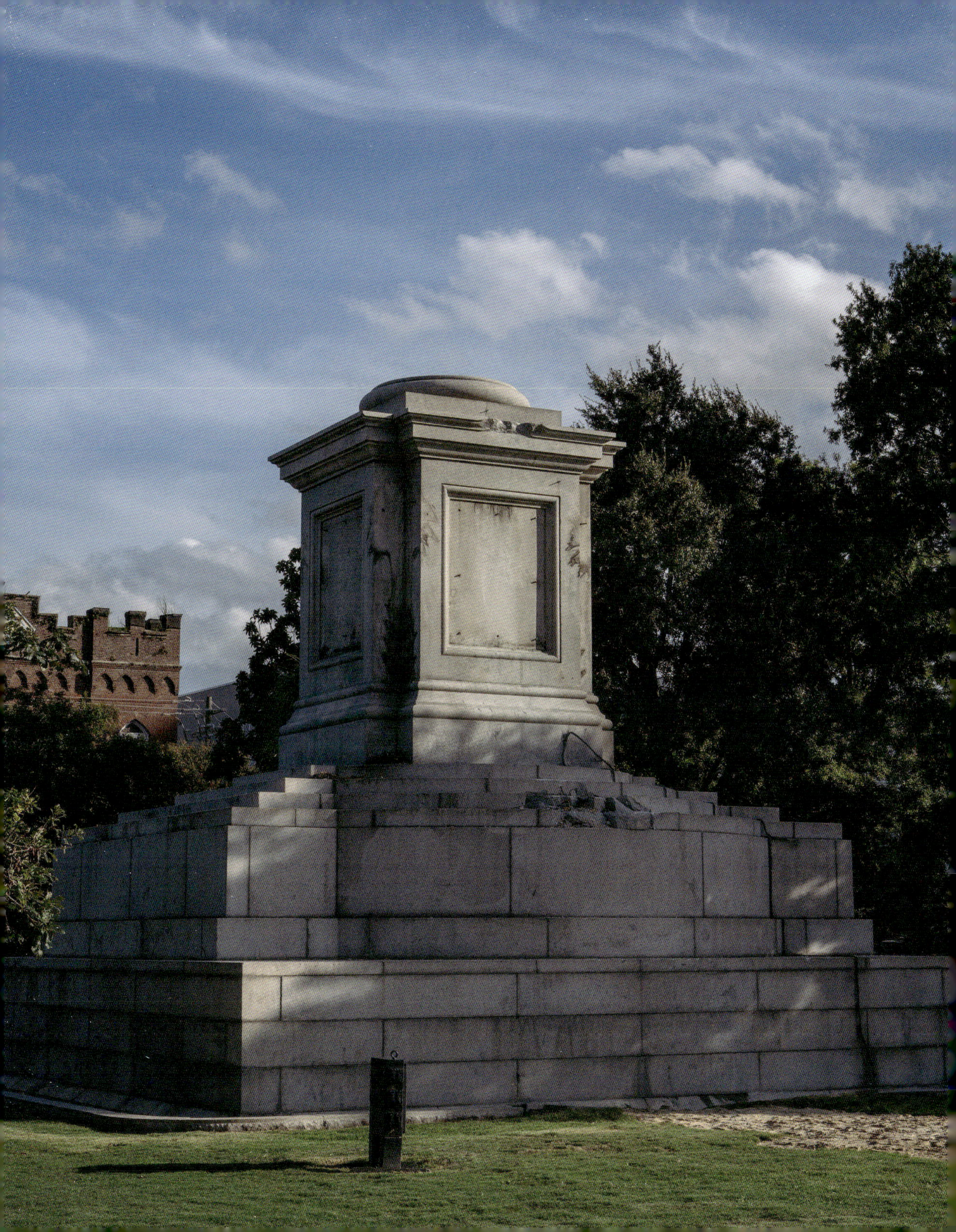

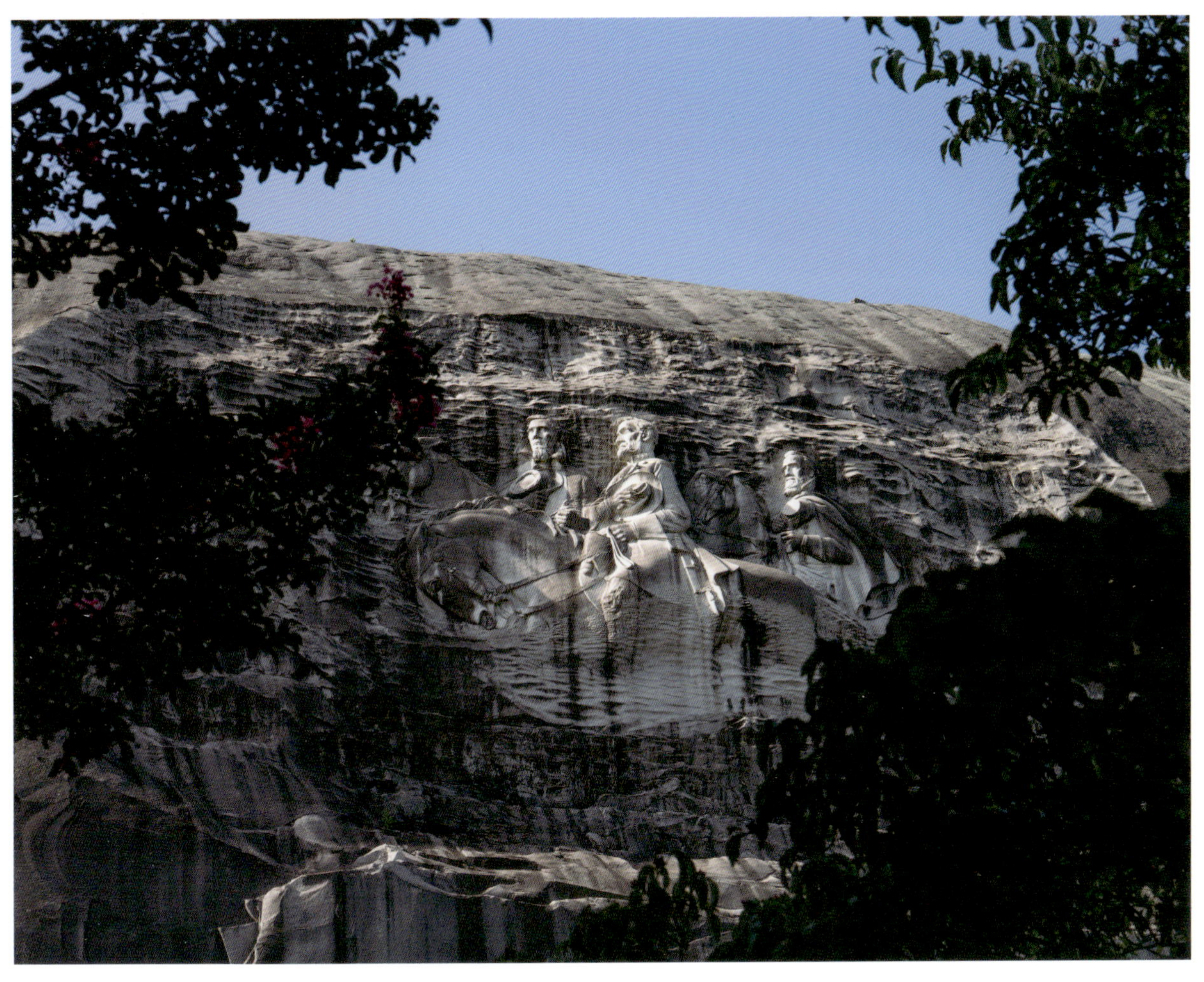

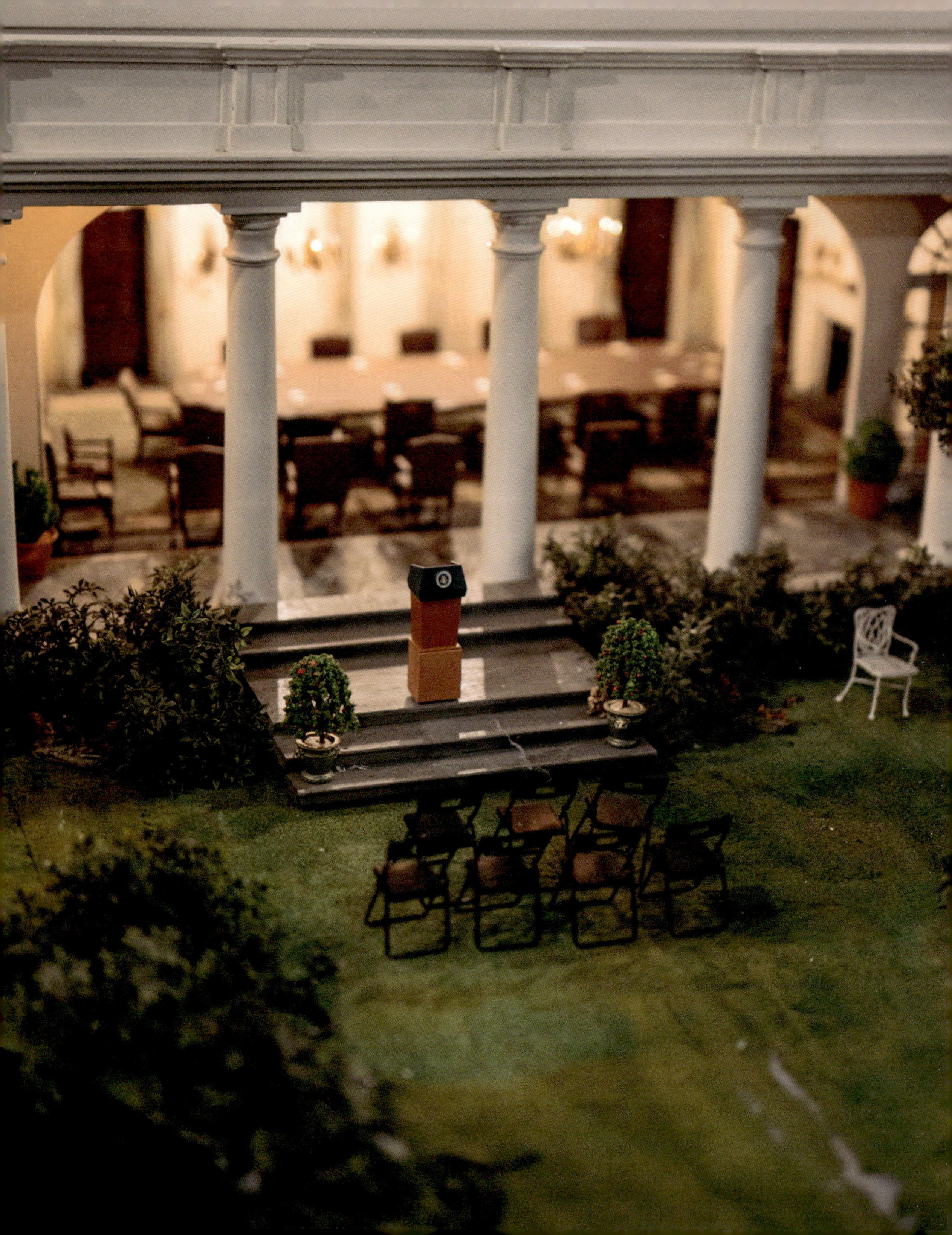

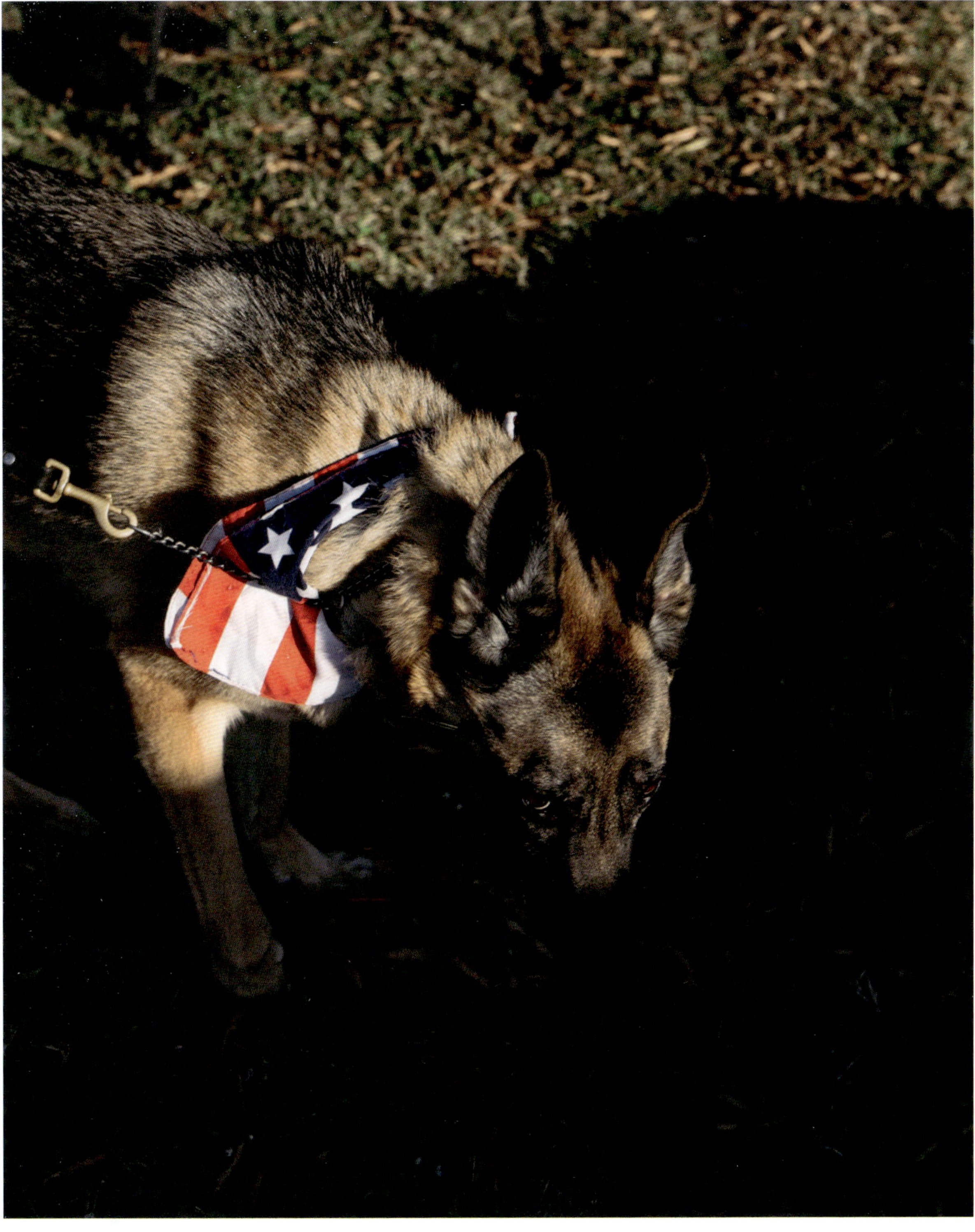

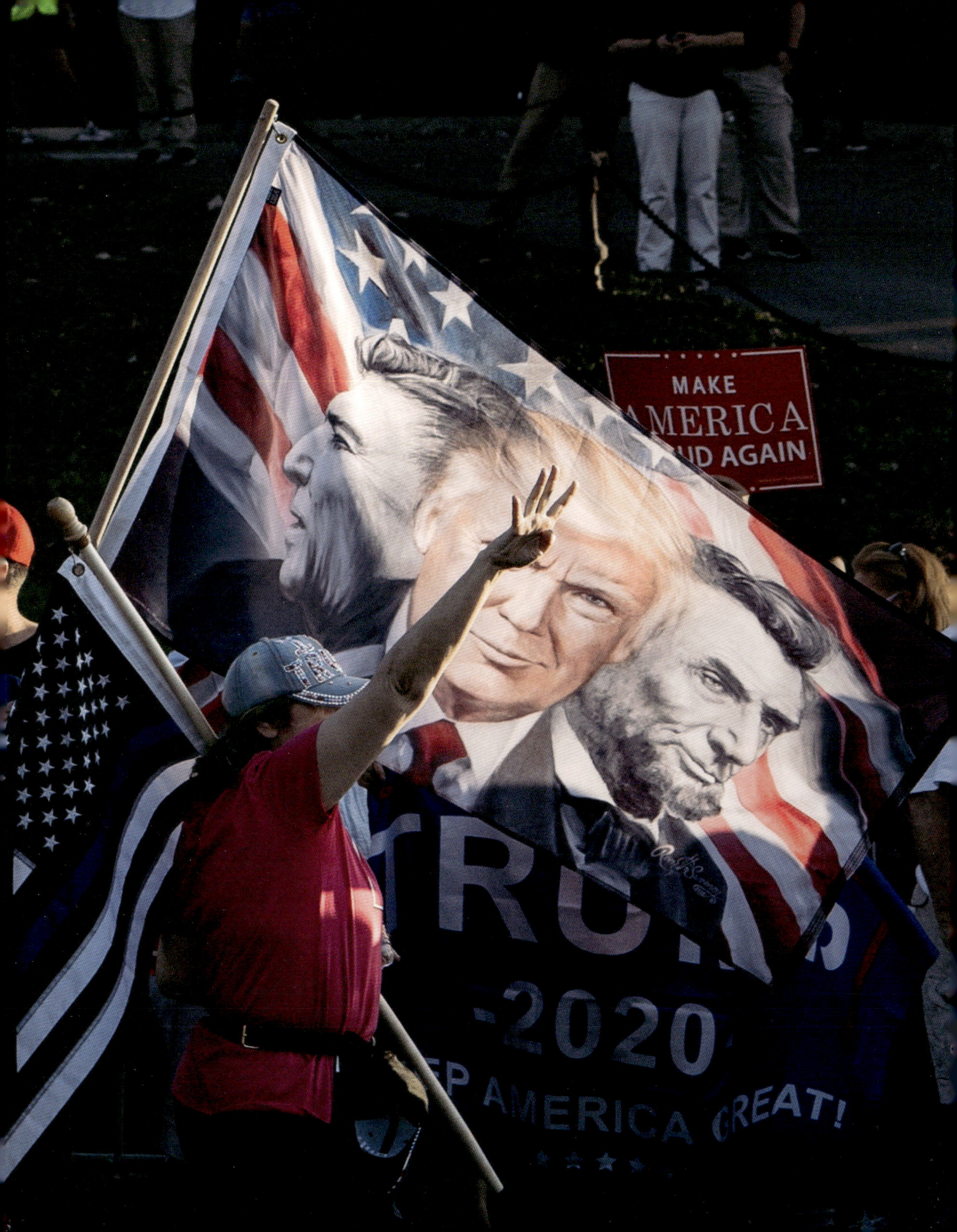

MAKE
AMERICA
AGAIN
2020
AMERICA

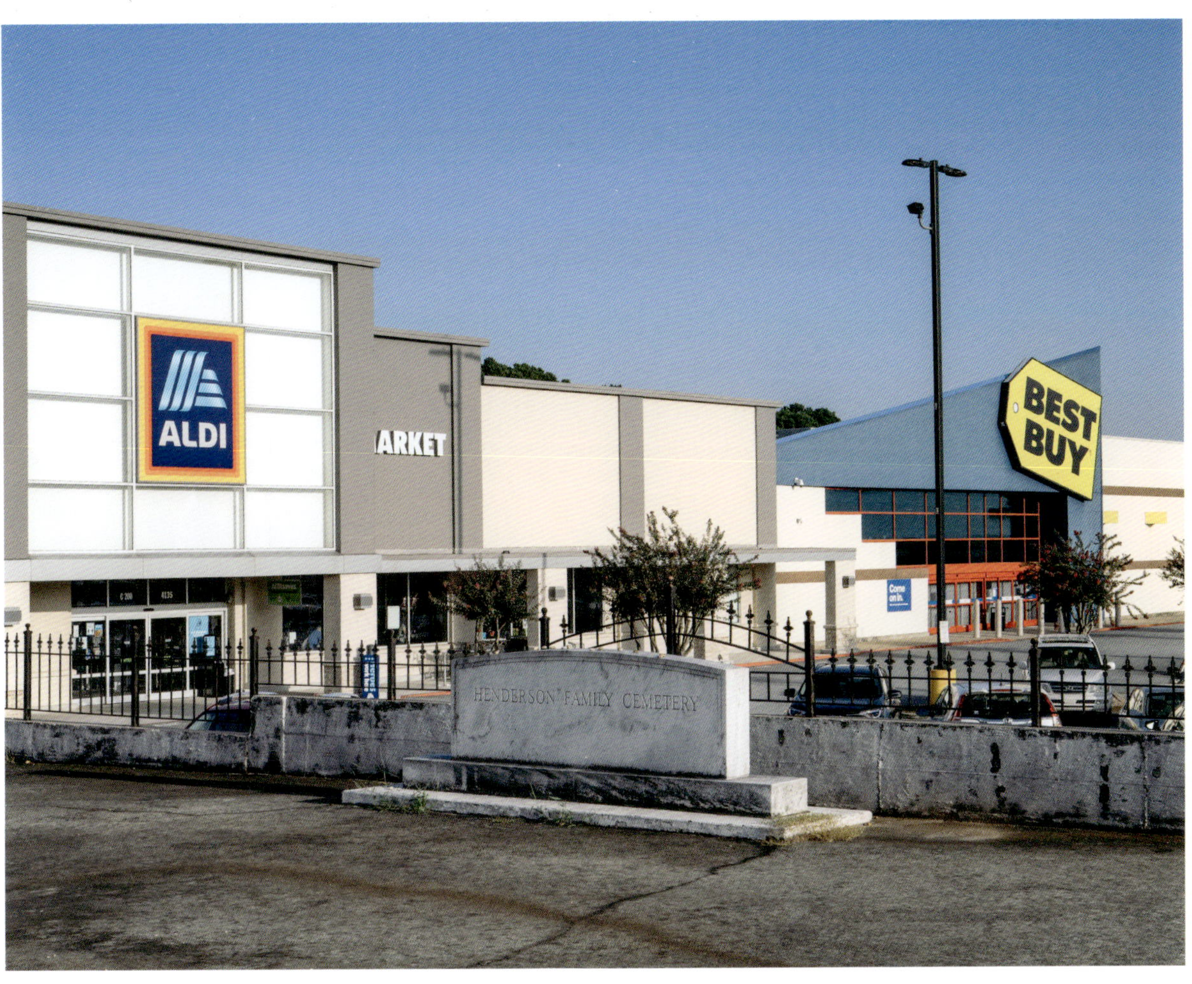
ALDI
ARKET
BEST BUY
Come on in.
HENDERSON FAMILY CEMETERY

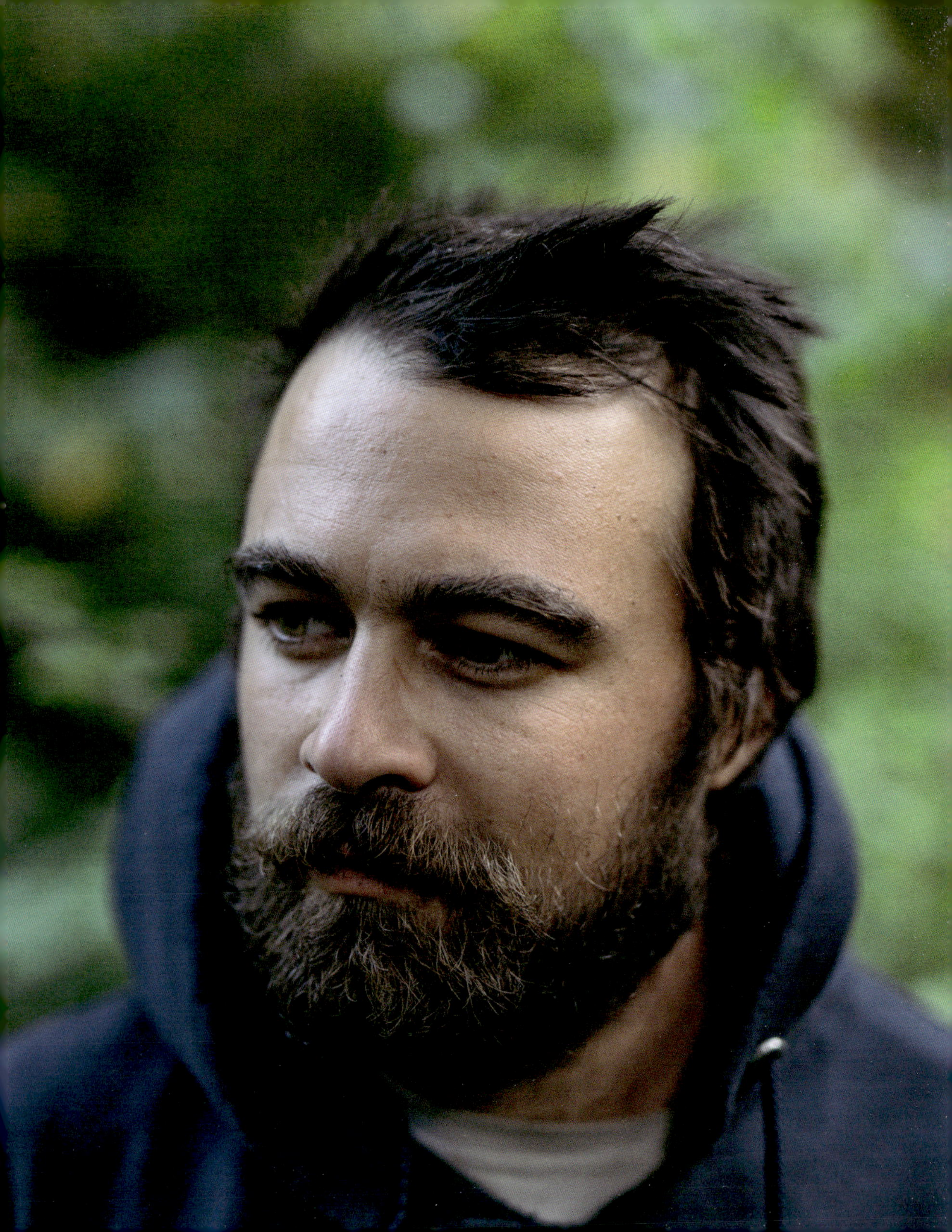

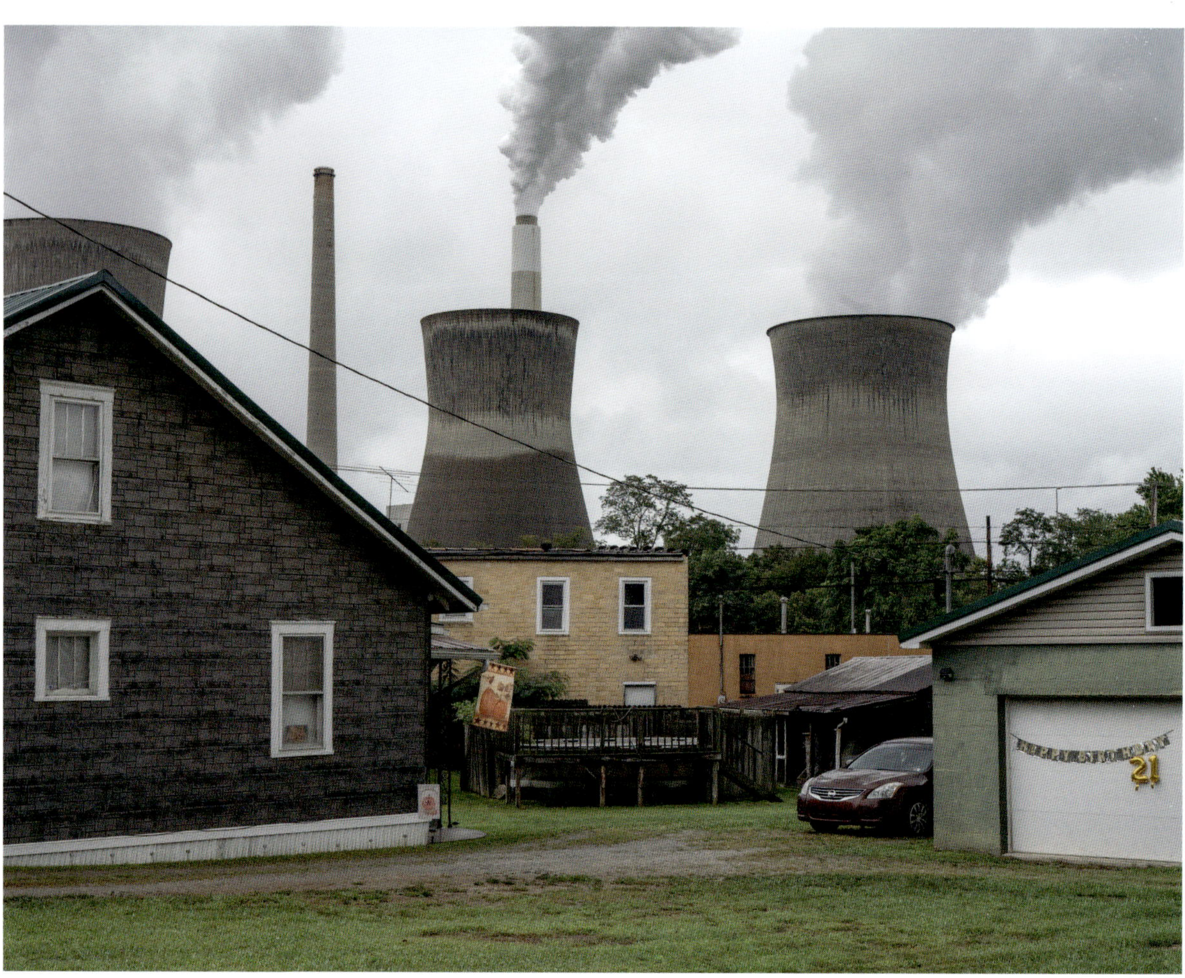
21

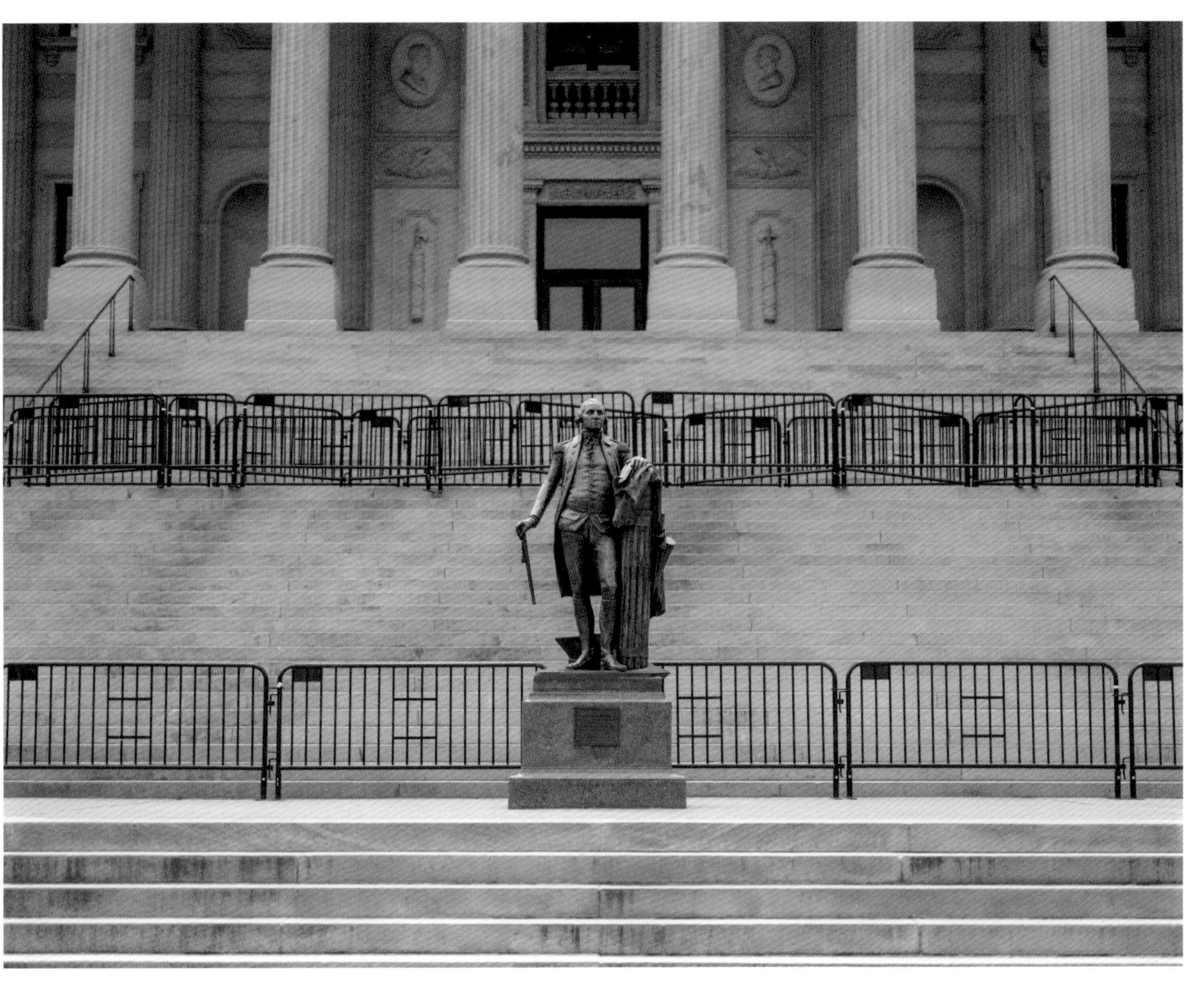

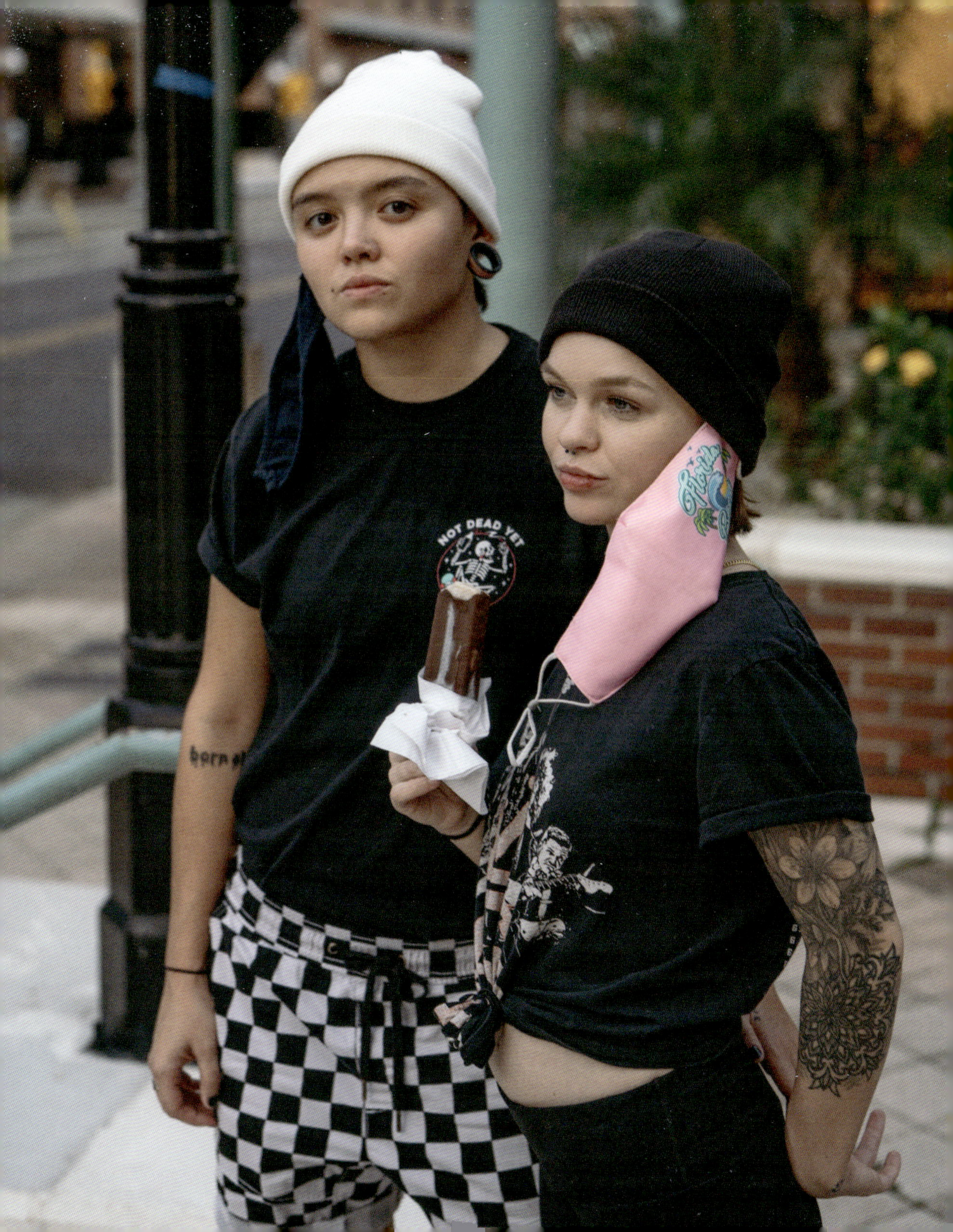
NOT DEAD YET

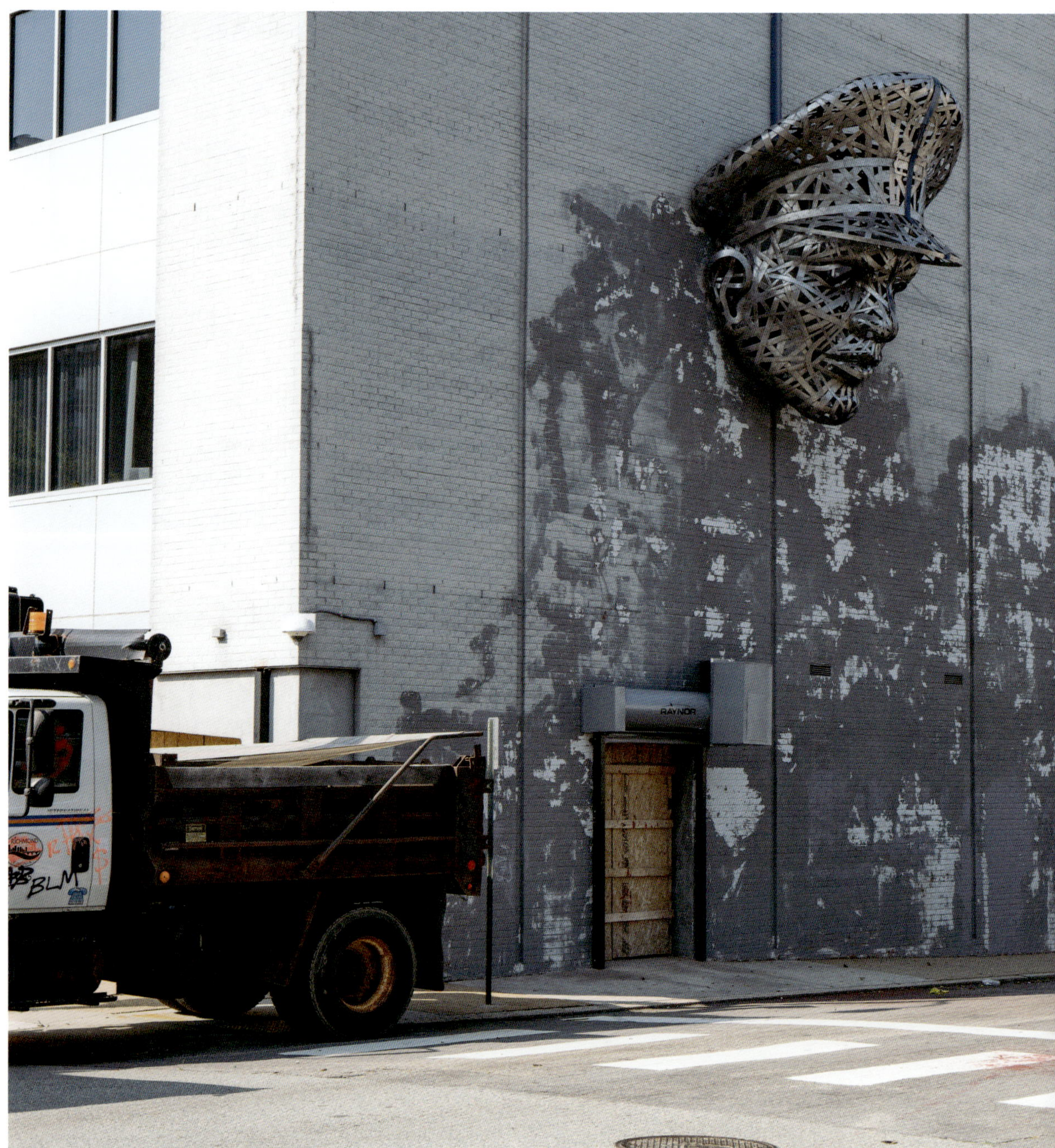
RAYNOR
BLM

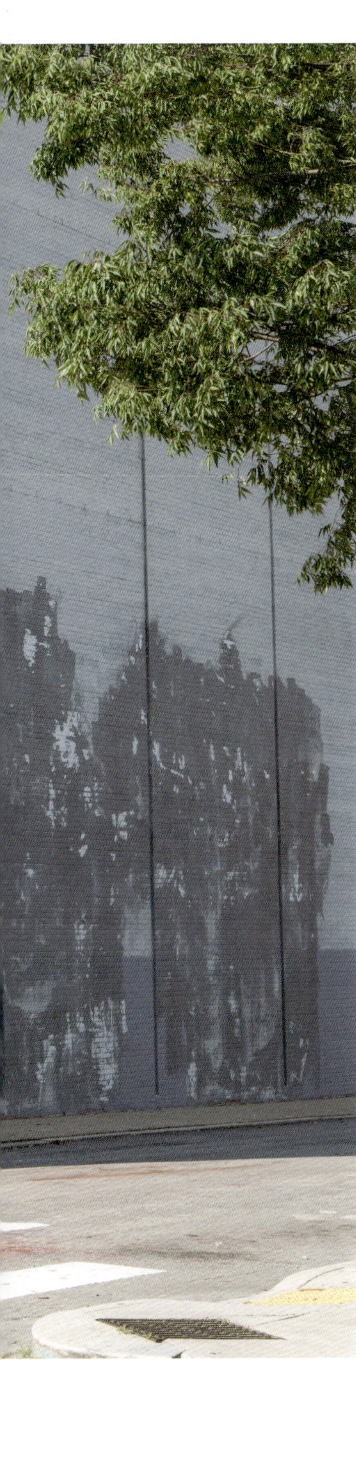

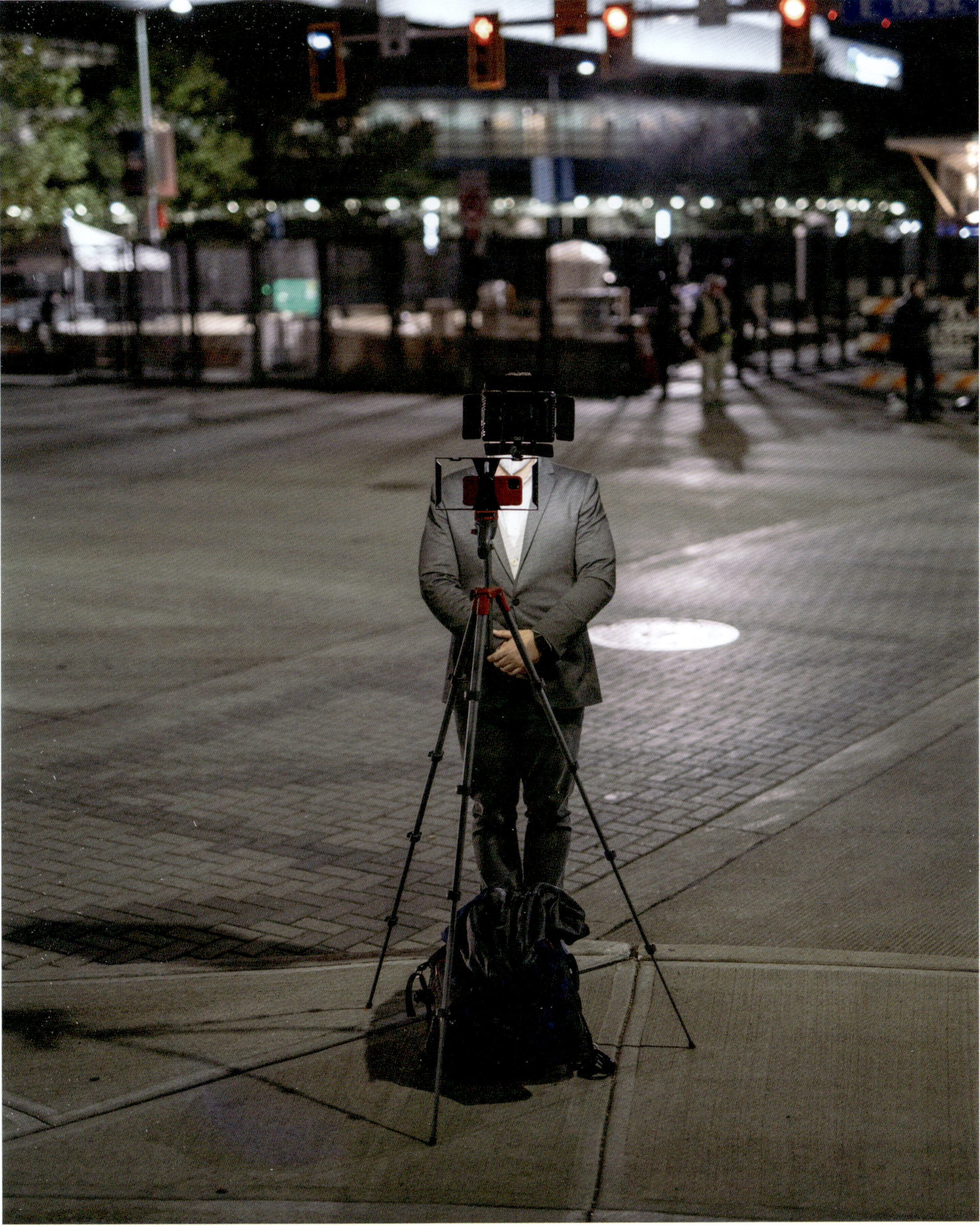

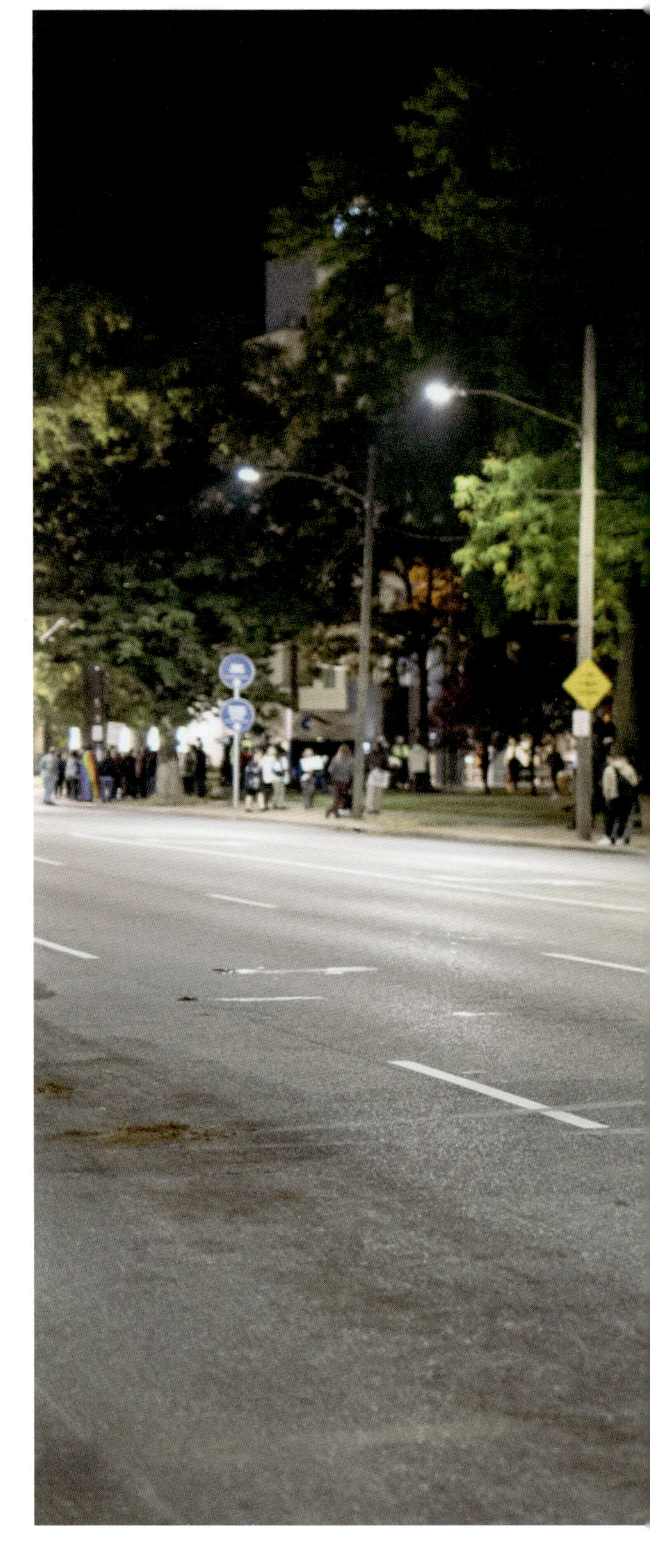

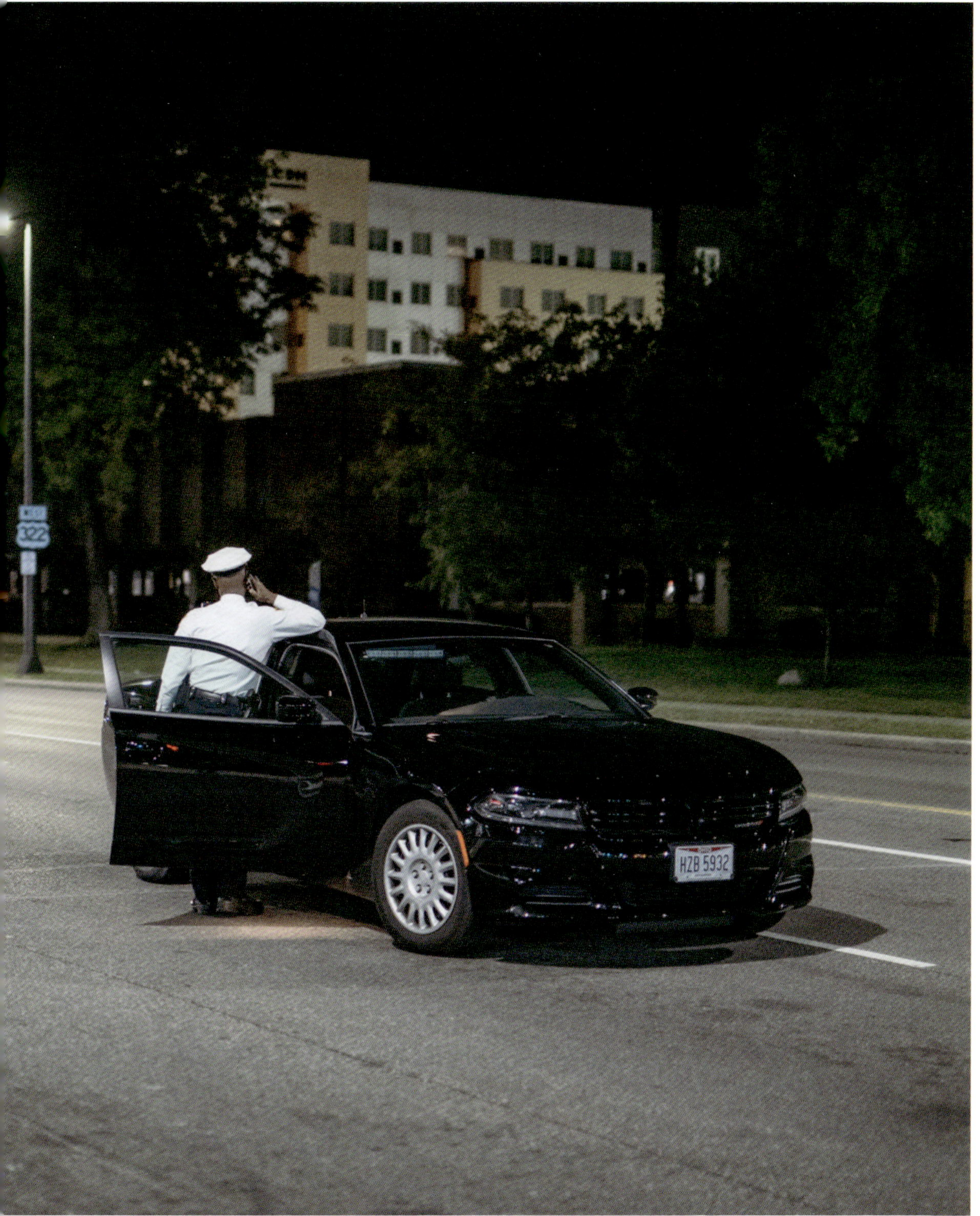
322
HZB 5932

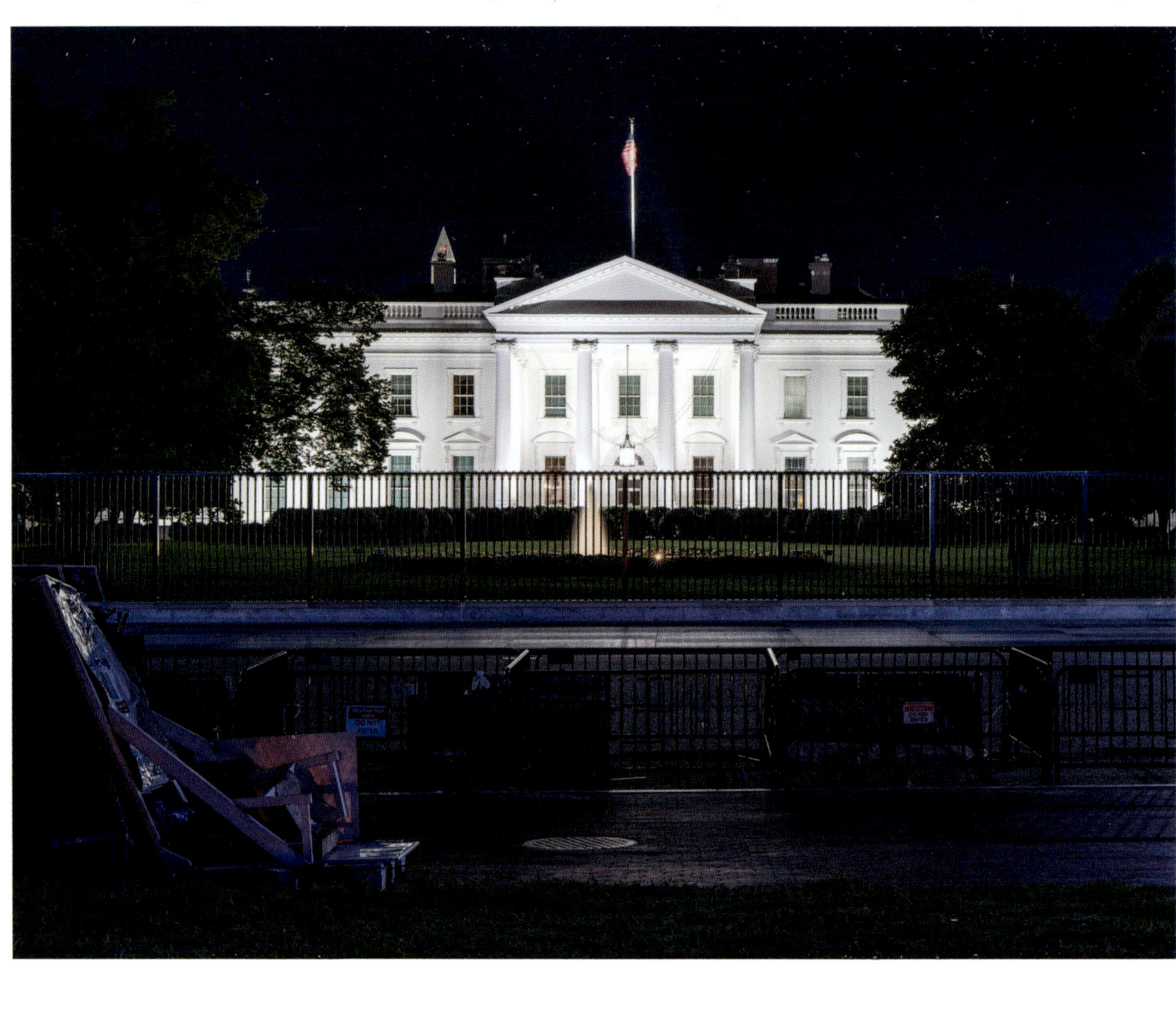

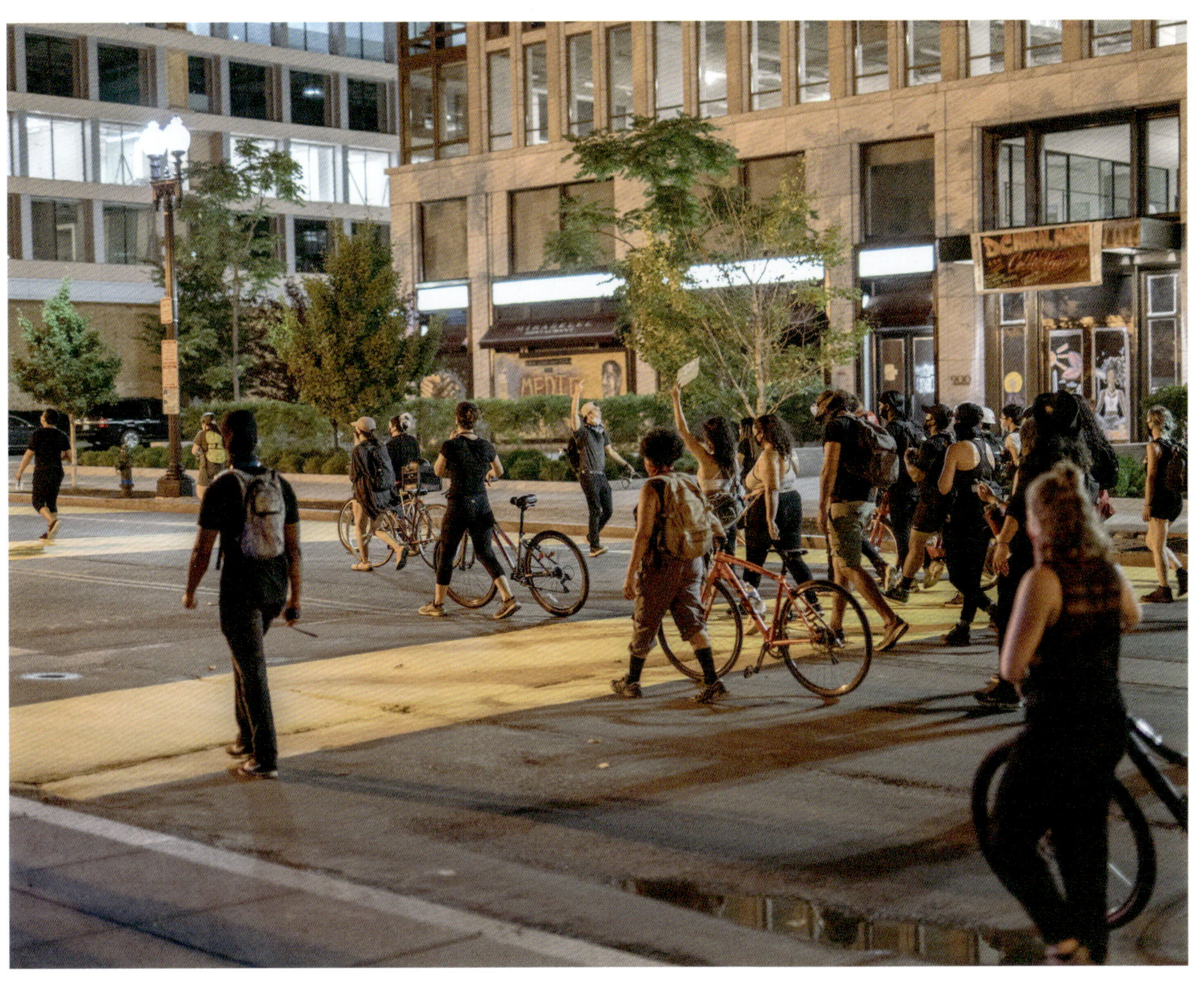

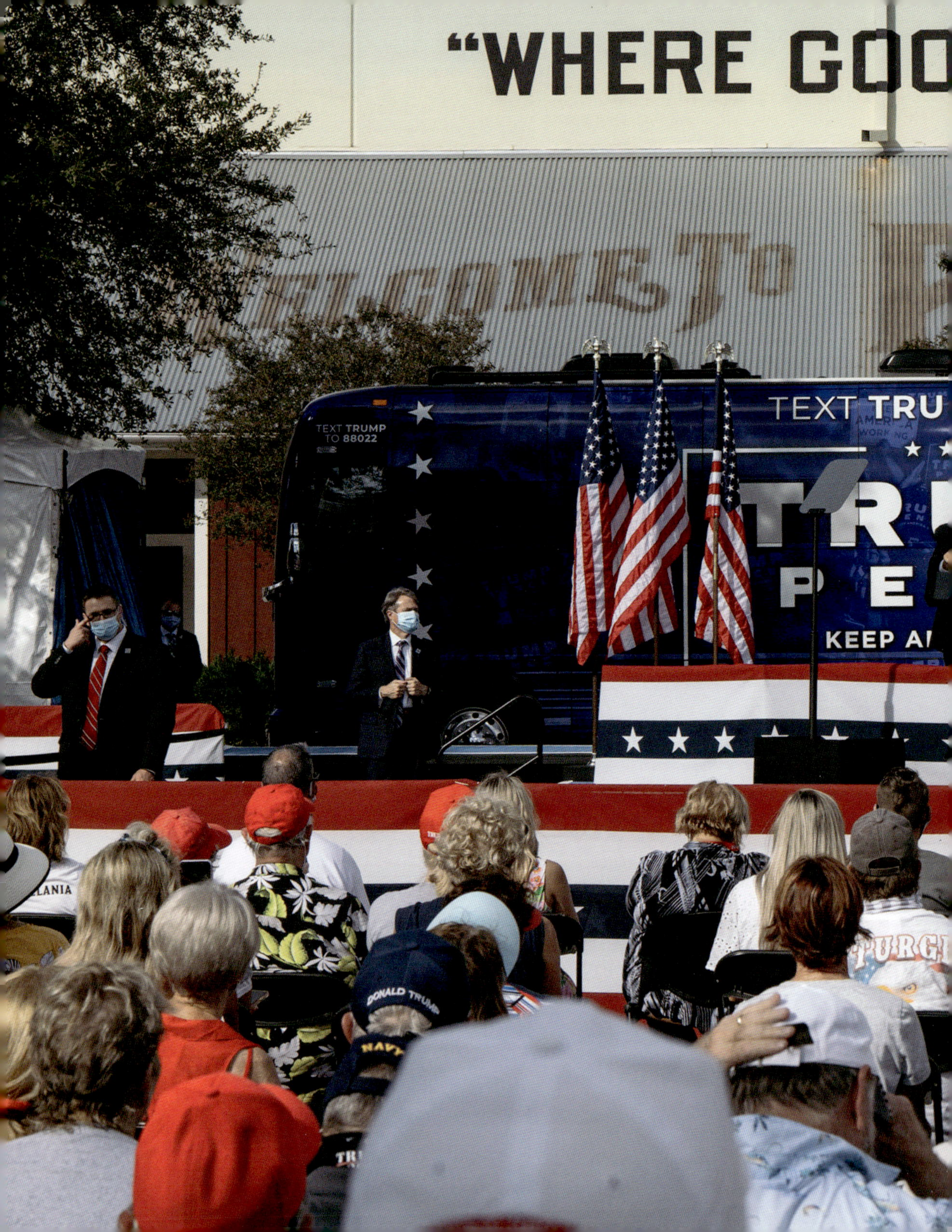
"WHERE GOO
TEXT TRUMP
TO 88022
TEXT TRU
KEEP A
DONALD TRUMP
NAVY

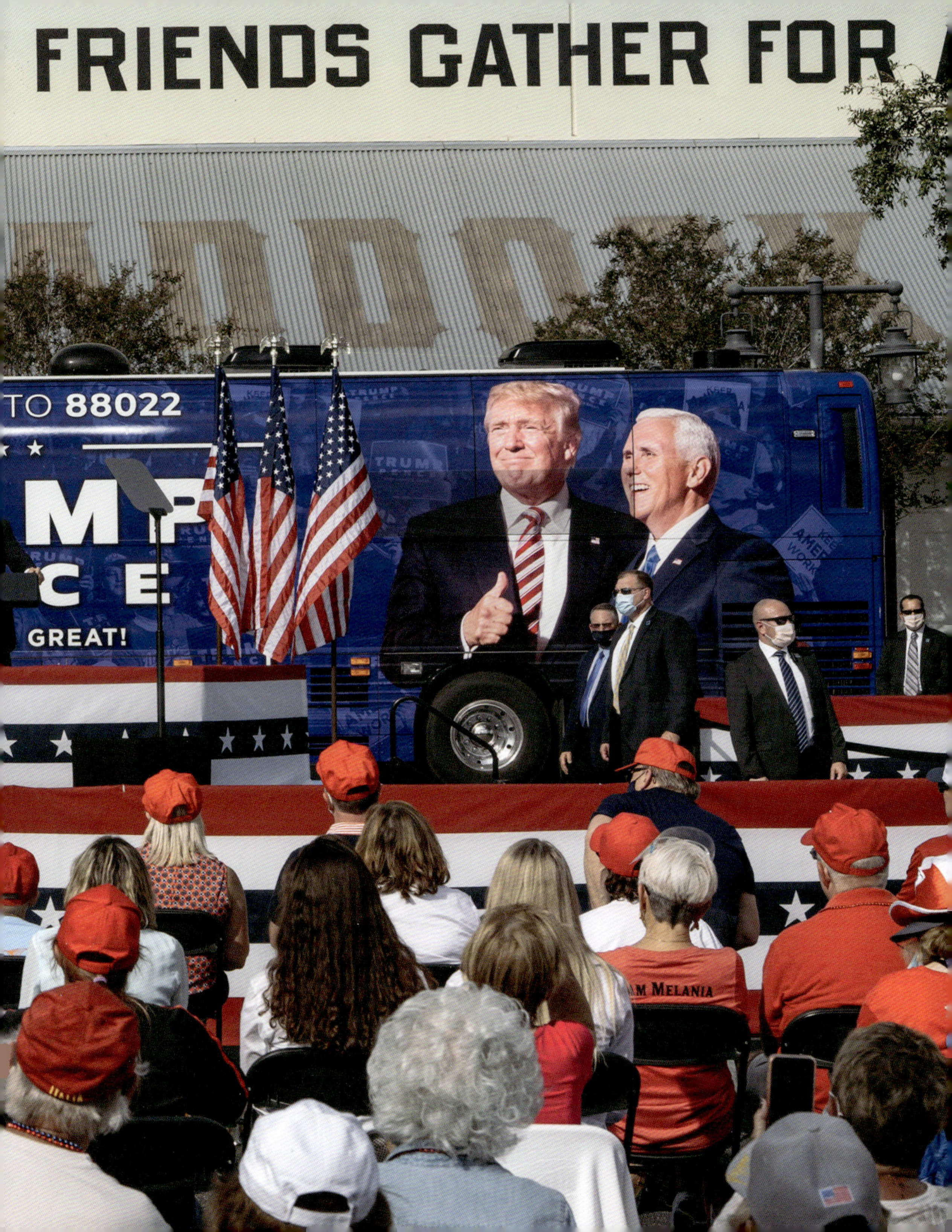

FRIENDS GATHER FOR
TO 88022
GREAT!
M MELANIA

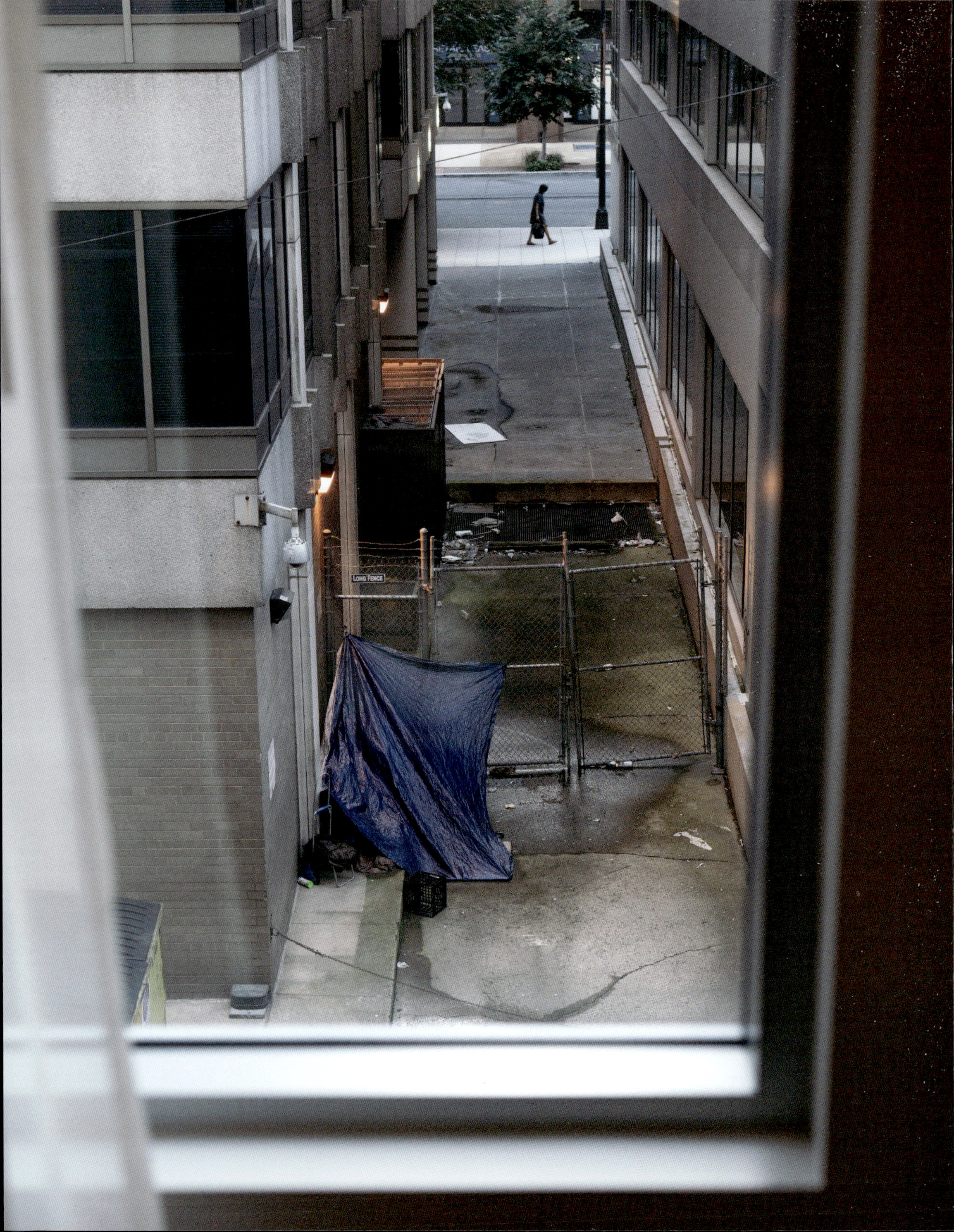
LONG FENCE

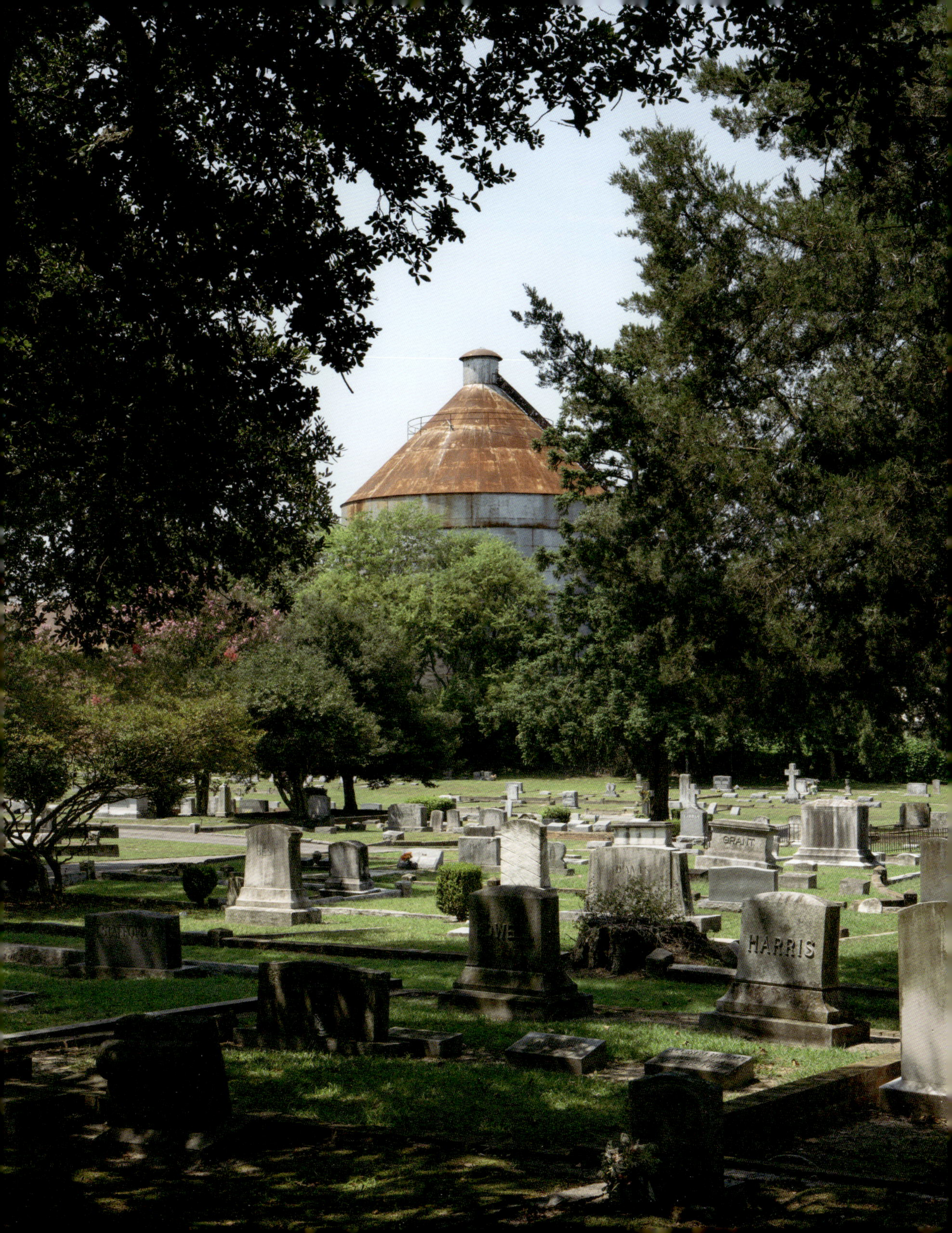
GRANT
HARRIS

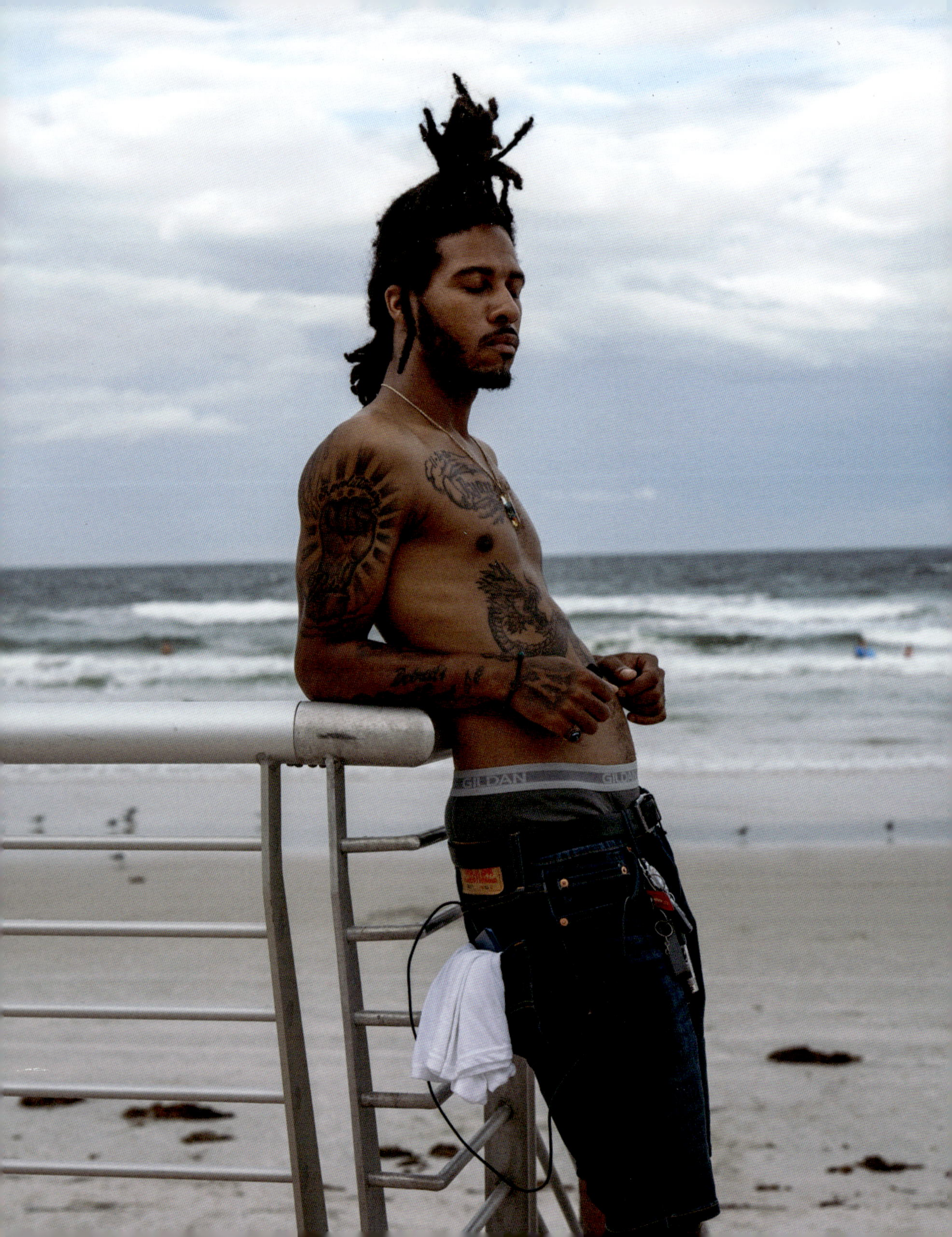
GILDAN
GILDAN

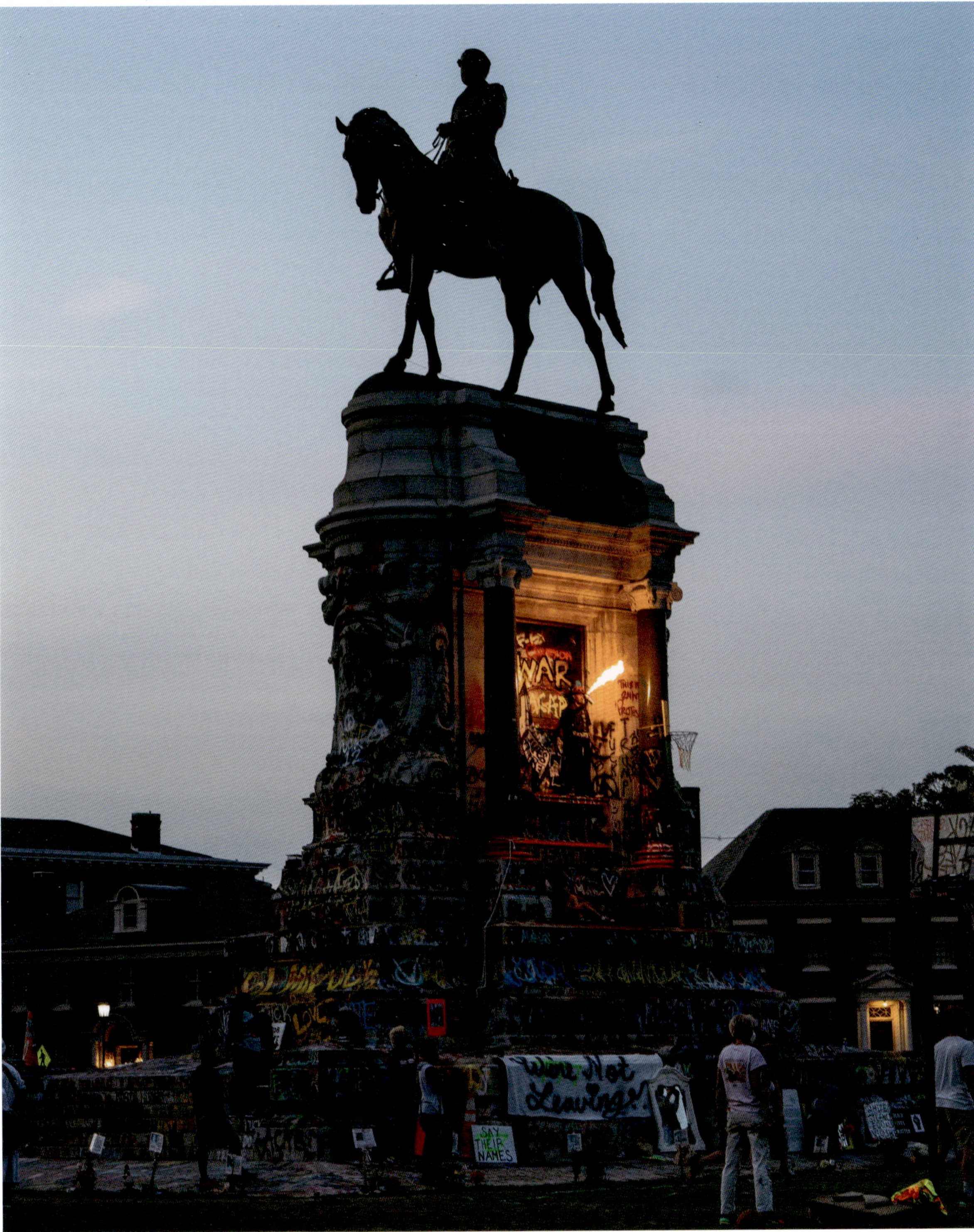
WAR
We're Not Leaving!
SAY THEIR NAMES

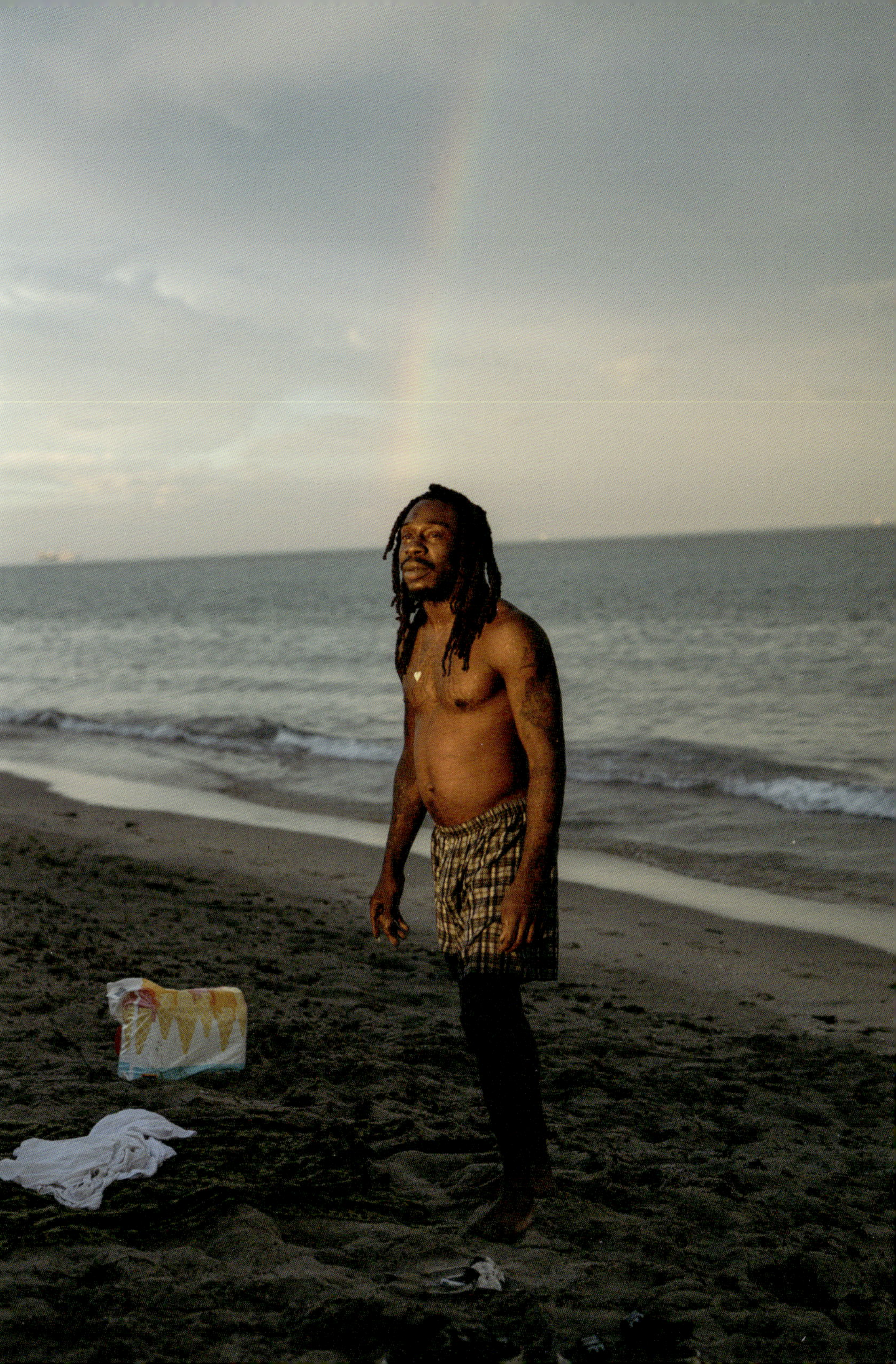

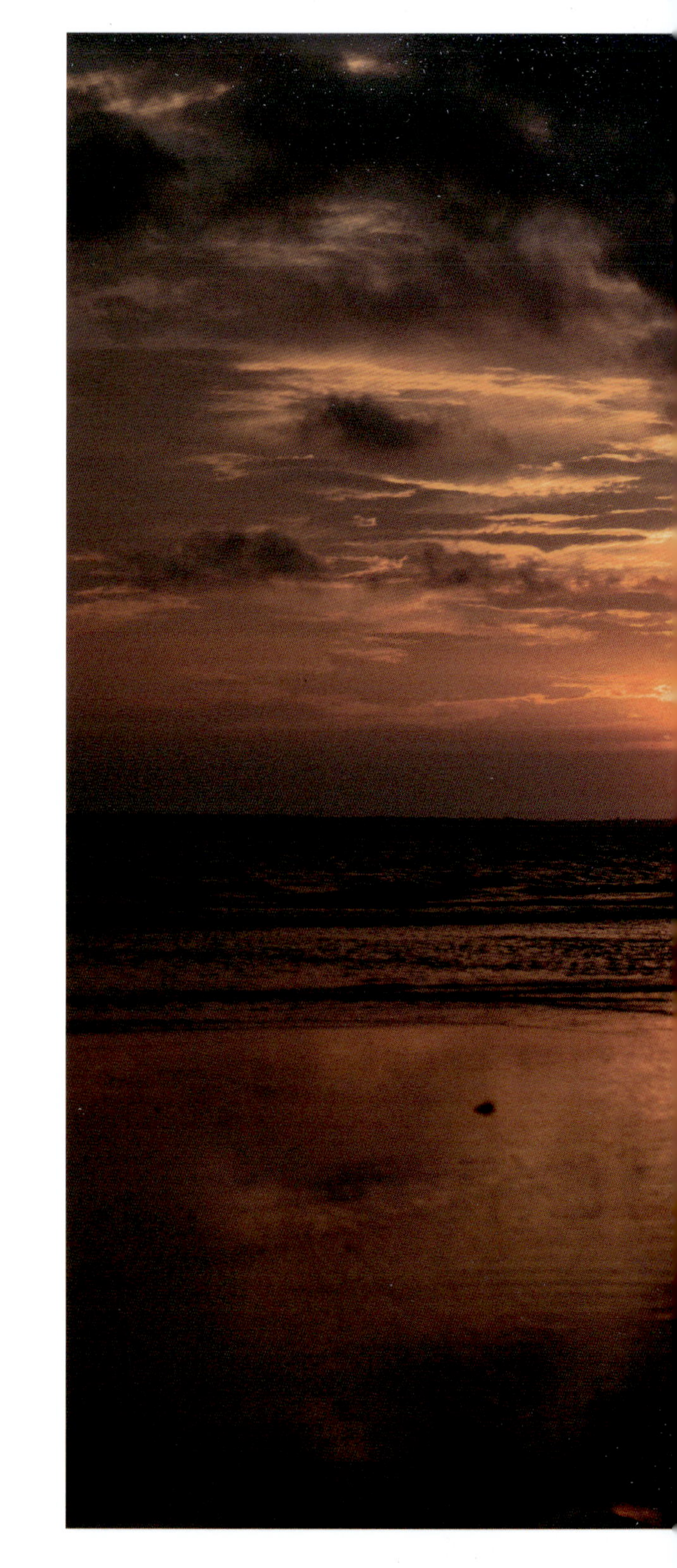

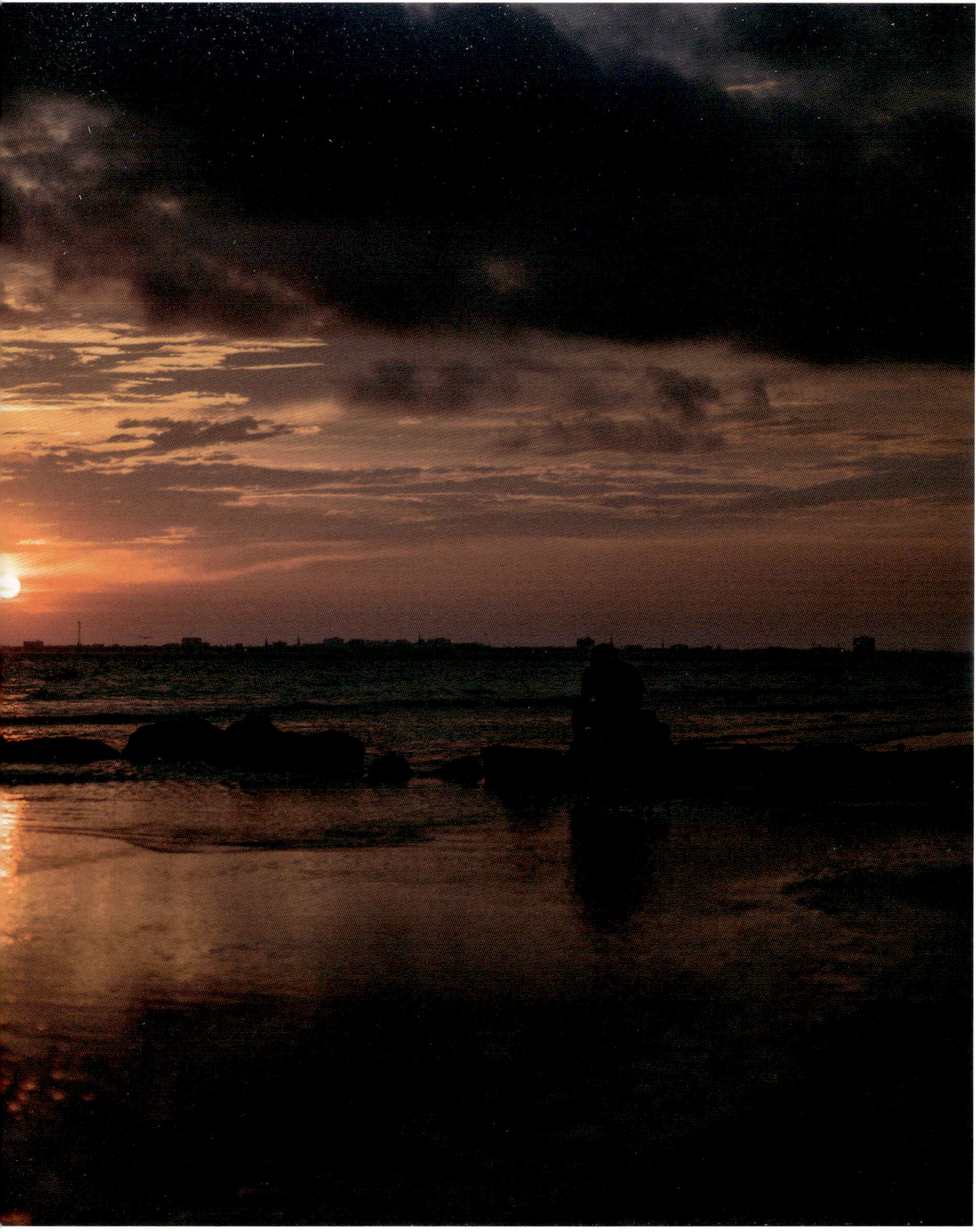